Contemporary Thoughts

on

Christian Higher Education

The University Year 1960-61

Pacific Lutheran University
Tacoma, Washington

378
P 119

CONTENTS

iii

INTRODUCTION

THE ACADEMIC YEAR 1960-61 was a significant one in the history of Pacific Lutheran University, Tacoma, Washington. The institution became a university with six academic units —College of Arts and Sciences, School of Business Administration, School of Education, School of Fine and Applied Arts, School of Nursing and Graduate School.

When the institution was founded on October 14, 1890, it was incorporated as Pacific Lutheran University. However, when the school opened for classes it was known as Pacific Lutheran Academy. In 1920 it became Pacific Lutheran College, the name under which it operated until 1960.

In recognition of this important step in the history of the university, a series of special events were held throughout the school year. Outstanding personalities from many areas on the American scene appeared as speakers. The stimulating, scholarly presentations of these leaders are significant contributions to contemporary thinking on Christian higher education. This book contains these vital addresses.

FOREWORD

The Small University in Christian Education

ON SEPTEMBER 1, 1960, Pacific Lutheran College returned to its original name, "Pacific Lutheran University." This name is inscribed on the cornerstone of our "Old Main Building" (now known as Harstad Hall).

Like many other such educational enterprises, our founders descended from their high mountain of hopes into deep valleys of despair. The way was rugged and the pathway was uncertain.

After nearly seventy years of trial and error, we are now using our original name, "Pacific Lutheran University." The name is properly changed and filed in the office of the Secretary of State at Olympia, Washington. The new beginning date coincided with the dedication period of the new Administration Building (October 14, 1960). On the brick front of that building, the name is permanently inscribed, "Pacific Lutheran University, Founded 1890." For about two years, the Administration and Faculty studied the new structure that has been employed in the University, beginning September of 1960. We are still working on the finished master plan, which will be the guide for the "University of Tomorrow."

YESTERDAY—THE SMALL COLLEGE

It has been said that yesterday was the day of the small college, while tomorrow will be the day of the small university. The small university is an institution which, by size, structure and diversity of function, stands between the large university and the small college. The small university will be less than 3,000, in contrast with the larger university, which will run far above that size. The small university will be distinctly less complex in administration and in the variety of programs and curricula.

Our "University" will have several distinct programs, or schools, or colleges, each serving a substantial number of students. We will attempt to hold the administrative structure somewhere between the single-purpose college and the multi-purpose university. We will offer the master's degree, but not the doctorate. We will expand our master's program as the needs and resources develop. We have already achieved national accreditation by the National Council on Accreditation of Teacher Education to grant the master's degree in education. We desire to meet the needs of our constituency within the limits of resources provided. It is very possible that the future will require a greater flexibility of purpose and of service. Students will continue to come to us from the Lutheran Church, the children of alumni, the community of Washington, and from around the world.

We must be prepared to meet a diversity of needs on the part of our students. We must be prepared to do this on a very high level of spiritual and academic excellence. The best will never be too good. If there is to be any difference, we must do a better job than ever before. This means better equipment and a scholarly faculty which would qualify for the staff of any large university.

A DIVERSIFIED PROGRAM

Our students of tomorrow will increasingly demand a diversity of programs. Some will require and demand a general education in the arts and sciences; others need an opportunity for professional specialization at the undergraduate level; others want a strong foundation for professional study at the graduate level; still others will want the services of a program of continuing education for adults. Since we are a Church-owned university, we are aware that, above all else, our "University" should aim to prepare its young men and women for Christian service. The Lutheran Church now grants us annual subsidies equal to the entire cost of operating the College in 1943-44. The Lutheran Church has been more generous with us in its financial support than has any other denomination in the West, including both Roman Catholic and Protestant colleges and universities. We must never lose sight of this interest as we live and serve in our University.

WE ARE A UNIVERSITY NOW

Already before September 1, 1960, we were a University. Through a preliminary self-study, we have reorganized so that our new administrative structure, as well as our curricula, is being established along the lines of a university, rather than those of a single-purpose college. In this change, we have been very careful not to take our teachers out of the classroom; we are carefully avoiding the danger of losing the closely-knit relationship between the schools or colleges involved in the University.

The curricular developments at our University have been so rapid that our friends hardly know what has happened. Sometimes it seems as if our own staff has not fully realized what has been going on. Our College of Arts and Sciences provides a liberal education. It is our purpose to see that this is in the best tradition, consistent with the finest in American education in today's world—and tomorrow's.

Our present program provides for five schools or colleges, and the graduate school, while the future is likely to hold the necessity for the establishment of other units which will enhance our usefulness to home, Church, state, and world.

SOME REASONS WHY WE CHANGED OUR NAME

With the rapidly expanding junior colleges, or community colleges, all over America, it is a real possibility that the senior colleges, or small universities, will develop a three-year sequence of studies beyond the junior college level, leading to the master's degree.

It will take a great deal of good communication to make our community, state and nation aware of the difference that exists between an institution such as Pacific Lutheran University and the junior college. It will be so easy for a potential student to say, "Why go to Pacific Lutheran University and pay tuition when we can go to a junior college and get an education without tuition?" Now that we are carrying the name "University," we are calling attention to the fact that we are not a junior college, nor are we just another ordinary college, but that we are an institution of outstanding academic excellence.

While we do not seek to become a big university, via enrollment, yet we do have a large enrollment. Actually, we are no longer a small college. During our University Year, we enrolled 2,350 different students within a twelve-month period.

Under our new University structure, we propose that we remain a small university while we will aim to retain as many as possible of our present small college values. It is quite certain that, even though we are ten times as big as we were in 1943, we have even more of the plus values. Our required daily Chapel service, our Student Congregation on a voluntary basis, the fine student activities, all contribute to this central joyous fact.

Some will say that it is better to be a "good college," rather than a "poor university." As we were a "good college" before September 1, 1960, so we will continue to remain increasingly and more vigorously a superior "small university."

NEW ADMINISTRATIVE POSITIONS

As we change to the new University structure, there will be some administrative positions and titles. The deans of our six schools will be teaching deans, assigned a number of hours in the classroom, together with their administrative duties.

We are confronted with a great challenge to leadership in the world of higher education, both in Church and State. We have a responsibility to assume a leadership which our resources and generation provide. We fully expect that at best, we will be in a state of experimentation for a long time, and that future developments may alter the institution's course with respect to specific aspects of the program. The fact is, who dreamed in 1943 that which we now see and experience? Our faculty has grown from about 19 to about 115 during the University Year. This will increase by nearly 10% during our second year as a University. Our student body has grown by more than ten times, and our resources have grown from $268,000 in 1943, to a new appraisal of more than $10,000,000; our buildings have increased from four to more than thirty, and our accreditation has placed us among the foremost schools in the land.

The University was established and is now maintained to serve distinctly Christian objectives. Therefore, this University, consistent with the Word of God and the Lutheran Confessions, seeks, by the Grace of God, to be at all times and in all places of its classroom and campus activities, distinctly and positively Christian. This means that every faculty and staff member and every student will be faced with a clear call to complete commitment to Jesus Christ for salvation and service. It is because of these objectives that we continue to give careful attention to our basic positions.

S. C. EASTVOLD

DR. C. CLEMENT FRENCH
President, Washington State University

DR. FRENCH gave the address at the convocation on October 14, 1960 celebrating the dedication of the Tacoma-Pierce Administration Building, the formal adoption of university status and the seventieth anniversary of the institution's founding.

Four Aims of the Human Spirit

MANY MONTHS AGO President Eastvold wrote me, generously asking that I take part in your program inaugurating your status as a university and dedicating certain new buildings on your campus. I checked his proposed date with my calendar and, with real reluctance, found that my answer had to be in the negative. Almost by return mail he came back with a proposal to revise the schedule and the invitation in such a way that I could take part. In doing this he not only put me in a position where a second refusal was both discourteous and impossible, but in actual fact gave me what I desired—a chance to accept his invitation and to meet with you at this time.

I had one primary reason both for appreciating the invitation and for wanting to accept it. Ever since I came to the State of Washington over eight and one-half years ago, the friendship and cooperation of my fellow-presidents throughout the entire State has been a real help to me. Early in my time in the State, I met President Eastvold and learned of the outstanding service he has rendered to higher education in the State in general and to education in the private church-related field in particular. One does not lightly decline the request of such a colleague.

In the second place, it is always a very real pleasure for me to come back again to your kind of campus. It is the type of campus on which I have spent the most of my academic life. While I am a graduate of a great Ivy League university in the East and taught there for eight years, the next nineteen years of my life as teacher and administrator were spent in a small church-related liberal arts college in Virginia. At that time thirty years ago, it had a student body of approximately six hundred and a faculty of 60. This is still its pattern of faculty and students. You knew them all, and while this was not usually an unmixed blessing, on balance I would say that it was a pleasure. The student body was homogeneous, and there were no problems of intercollegiate athletics to wrestle with. Likewise there was a common thread of genuine Christian concern and expression throughout the life of the college. Only eleven years ago did I leave that pattern of education for the much greater complexity of large university public administration. Each certainly had its place, and each must continue strong and active in our educational pattern if our society is not to suffer.

I say this at this point simply to indicate something of the background of my own experience and to show not only that I am aware of the position and the problems of the small church-related college, but to have you see why the chance to return for a brief time to such a campus is one that I would not lightly refuse.

There was another reason why I was anxious to accept this invitation. This morning as you dedicate this building,

2

you recognize the concern of many people for the ongoing of higher education in this institution. Our whole educational pattern is only as strong as the weakest part. Support for you and understanding of your problems means support for all of us and a better understanding of the problems of all of us. I join with President Eastvold in expressing deep appreciation to all who helped make this day possible. May this building and what has gone into it, both in money and in effort, be an inspiration to many others.

NATIONAL OBJECTIVES

Eleven months before we joined our Allies in World War II, President Roosevelt had formulated the long-range objectives of our country in a speech to the Congress on January 6, 1941:

"In the future days, which we seek to make secure, we look forward to a world founded upon four essential human freedoms.

"The first is freedom of speech and expression—everywhere in the world.

"The second is freedom of every person to worship God in his own way—everywhere in the world.

"The third is freedom from want—which, translated into world terms, means economic understandings which will secure to every nation healthy, peaceful life for its inhabitants—everywhere in the world.

"The fourth is freedom from fear—which, translated into world terms, means a world-wide reduction of armaments to such a point and in such a thorough fashion that no nation will be in a position to commit an act of aggression against any neighbor—anywhere in the world."

Through the life of our country, we in the colleges have been concerned with these four aims of the human spirit, with some varied emphasis depending on our type of institution. The first of these freedoms aimed to secure for man the release from the restraints on the free use of that power which distinguished him from a beast—to give him *intellec-*

3

tual freedom. The second was the expression of the desire of man for *religious freedom*—the freedom to think for himself in matters of the spirit and to worship God in his own way.

The third was *economic freedom*—the desire that man so develop the control of the powers of nature that life might become more abundant—freer and happier. And in the fourth was sought *political freedom*—the chance for man to be his own master in an ordered and free society, where the state existed for man and not man for the state.

While mankind has always been concerned to a degree with struggling towards these ends, I think that real progress in attaining the goals has been made only within the last three or four hundred years. And surely no perfect pattern nor final answer has been found as yet. But, I suggest that, here in this country of ours, there has been found the best testing ground for the ways to reach our goals. Our forefathers came to a new land, rich in potential, but one which tested to the limit the ability to master it. They were free of the traditional shackles of the old countries in clerical control, free to try new theories of government, and free to explore the truth, wherever it might lead them.

And to one who, as I, grew up on the Eastern seaboard, and has lived both in the Southwest and the Pacific Northwest, the continuance here in the West of that pioneer spirit today is very apparent. There is still out here the attitude which says, "I will judge a man for himself and his abilities" and "I will try a new way if it seems better than the old way." This is the opportunity which we have in this country—and have had from the days of our Founding Fathers.

As I see it, the college has had the opportunity, through its whole life in this country, to promote these four aspirations of the human mind. It is still the chief function of the colleges and universities—certainly of a college such as yours. May I consider briefly the role of the college in these four areas of freedom—though in a different order than the President listed them.

4

The move toward economic freedom has been one in which the threads have been tangled. The control of the forces of nature, the production of material things, and the learning to use them wisely and to man's best ends, have in part developed outside the college and university walls. Much has been given us by pragmatic inventors rather than by trained engineers—by men who never looked inside a college. Edison made his first successful lamp by trying hundreds of filaments until at last one was successful. Morse with his telephone and Ford with his automobile, alike, came to an end result by pragmatic rather than by theoretical approaches. But, these are examples from our pioneer heritage rather than from our scholastic tradition.

Against these, we can set a Steinmetz in pure research, a Urey or a Fermi in the university with his theoretical research which led to material result. And all of these material developments do not lead to a necessarily better economic life. Man can be so enveloped by things which he cannot distribute or use that he does not have a better—rather a worse—economic life, as a result. Economic freedom does not lie in gadgets alone. It comes from their wise use. And in the development of means both to control the forces of nature and to study the economic adjustment of society to these new things, our colleges and universities are responsible for the training of young men and women to the end that economic forces may be balanced and adjusted to lead to a life more abundant, freer, and happier.

POLITICAL FREEDOM

In the area of political freedom, your college and mine have a major responsibility. We Americans have shown the world that a government of the people, by the people, and for the people can work. We admit the faults of our system, but we still hold to the proposition that the end of government is to protect the good life of the people—not to set up a mon-

5

ster for which the people exist. This struggle never ends and is possibly more acute today than in any other period of our history. In it, the college man plays a preeminent part, as he always has. Jefferson, Madison, and Marshall were all college men. "I shudder for the future of democracy," Jefferson once said, "when the people are not educated." And Washington wrote, ". . . in proportion as the structure of government gives force to public opinion, it is essential that public opinion should be enlightened." That enlightenment still has far to go, but that is our task, and we shall not shirk it. It is of primary importance, second only to the task of the Church, that we should produce trained thinkers to carry a sane, sensible, and effective government.

Religious liberty

In the area of religious liberty, the college has had a clear and dominant role. No field of human thought has been so filled with errors and superstitions as theology. A friend of mine in Virginia once added a companion phrase, which I liked, to the familiar one, "the blood of the martyrs is the seed of the Church," when he said, "and heresy has been its safeguard." It has been heresy which, in an ecclesiastical sense, has led to clear thinking in a confused area. Without it, medieval religious thought would still be fostered in our churches of today. I am no heretic—unless you Lutherans consider an Episcopalian as such, *per se*. I mean only that our colleges, in fostering the thinking process, inevitably have led to a heterogeneity of thought which has been bad for traditionalism but good for religious progress and development.

Freedom of the mind

None of us would question, I am sure, the importance of these three freedoms: economic, political, or religious. And yet, I wonder whether, in our role of college men, the fourth

6

freedom of the human mind is not to us the most important, the one which guarantees all the others—the right to think for oneself. When used wisely, it protects all our freedoms and makes us a little lower than the angels. We might well place over the gateway of every college, as a constant guide to our efforts, the words of Thomas Jefferson, "I have sworn on the altar of God eternal hostility to every form of tyranny over the mind of man."

I need not over-emphasize to you that through our history the chief means of developing this intellectual freedom has been our American system of education; our bulwark in this struggle has been the college. Our educational system has its roots deep in the tradition of Western Europe from which the bulk of our people came. It began shortly after the settlement of the Western Hemisphere. Harvard College was established in 1636, The College of William and Mary in 1693, and Yale in 1701. These institutions and others made a major contribution to the developing life of a pioneer country. They were the source of the clergy and the political leaders of their time, and their significance must not be underestimated. It may well be said that our American system of constitutional government and our American system of higher education are the two major developments of the American people.

We have seen a steady development in the pattern of that American system of higher education. I do not need to remind you that the college in our country grew out of the Church. It grew out of the desire and the determination of religiously concerned peoples to protect and develop our faith in God. Was it not Yale which included in its Charter as part of its purpose—the protection of the people from an uneducated clergy?

But the development of higher education in this country has introduced another note which at times today leads to confusion and misunderstanding. Bearing in mind the Western European tradition and the religious tradition, it became evident by 1800, however, that a higher educational system, *solely* classical and traditional, did not relate ade-

7

quately to all the needs of a rapidly expanding and developing nation nor to the occupations of the mass of the people.

I shall not detail the rise of the state universities, the land-grant colleges, the urban universities, and the junior colleges. The people had spoken and said that education of more than a small fraction of their children was what they wanted. No longer was higher education to be restricted to the aristocracy. Instead, it was to be made available to those of the masses who might profit by it—and by that profit, make a new kind of society here from that their fathers had left overseas. At long last, Jefferson's definition of a university as "an institution in which every branch of knowledge useful at this time is taught to the highest degree" became real.

I said that in this development the *simpler* structures of the seventeenth and the eighteenth centuries were left behind by the wish of the people. What do they wish in our system? I mention only a few of the things I think they expect.

EQUAL OPPORTUNITY

In the *first* place, they wish an equal opportunity for every young person, within the limits of his intellectual ability, to develop those abilities to the ultimate. In the Declaration of Independence, our Founding Fathers expressed a belief, the wording of which may need to be slightly changed, but which seems to me inherent in this expectation. They said, "We hold these truths to be self-evident, that all men are created equal." While we must admit that all men are *not* created equal, we are unwilling to admit in our democracy that all men should not have an equal opportunity within the limits of their ability. Holding to this belief, our people would say that it is proper to provide this equal opportunity. They would agree that a considerable part of the cost of education should be borne from public funds, but that everyone should be expected to have a share in the cost of his own education.

8

In the *second* place, most people would say that the ultimate responsibility for the control of education should be in the hands of the people through their representatives. Methods differ as to how these representatives shall be obtained. The precise nature of their responsibility varies. Yet, in a democratic society where education is considered to be a concern of the people, the responsibility for its control must ultimately come back to the people, themselves.

In the *third* place, the people expect that an institution should provide the opportunity for carrying on research—research that is not slanted to a particular end; research to find the true answers to questions, not the answers that a group may desire.

I think they also expect a curriculum which does more than teach their sons and daughters how to make a living; they expect them trained in a particular specialty, but they also desire that, with the practical, we add the liberalizing areas of knowledge which enrich and envitalize a man.

EDUCATION FOR CITIZENSHIP

What they want is not merely a trained technician. They want a trained technician, a trained lawyer, a trained engineer, who at the same time is trained to take his place in a democratic society where each man, if democracy is to work, carries his share in being the master of his country. In other words, they require of us that we include in our education training for responsible citizenship in a democratic government.

And, *finally*, I think they insist that, for those who do not wish to participate in such a public educational experience but who may wish a special kind of educational pattern, for whatever the reason may be, under sectarian or non-public control, there should be a free opportunity, completely unhampered, to have their own experience put into practice.

I wonder if this is not the system we really have at the moment—unplanned, yes, and yet, as is true in so many

9

phases of our life and our government in our democratic society, we have stumbled through by trial and error to an end product which substantially meets the dreams and desires of the people. If it be questioned whether the people should have anything to do with its control, the answer lies in our concept of the democratic process. In a democracy, the people are the government; the people are those who set our pattern and who should set it. If we come to the time when we deny not only the *right*, but the *propriety*, of their setting that pattern, then I think we have come to the time when we deny the valid basis on which a democratic society rests.

Conflict inexcusable

You will note that I listed (and I believe this sincerely) that one of the expectations of the people is that a private, sectarian college shall be the right of any child who wants it. There are those, both in public and in private education, who would encourage conflict between the two great parts of education in America. To me, such an attitude is inexcusable. We have all kinds of people in a great country such as ours. No one pattern of education could possibly satisfy all. The variety of possible experiences available in our complex system meets the needs of our steadily increasing college population. There are those who say that every child is entitled to college admission. I disagree. But I hope that the day may come—for our people and our country will gain thereby—when every child who can *profit* by higher education may be admitted to an institution which will meet his needs. Note that this is not the same as the admission of all applicants. But conflict between colleges is needless. The task is greater than all of us working together can meet.

For nineteen years, as I have said, I taught chemistry and was an administrative officer in a small Virginia women's college. We required at least three years of Latin for entrance, three years of mathematics, two years of a modern foreign language. We required three years of foreign language toward the degree, three years of laboratory science, and a year of Bible—and *we excluded men.*

I am sure this pattern sounds strange out here, but five hundred girls applied each year for the two hundred places available. When, as Dean, I had protests about the required year of Bible or the required year of personal health and hygiene, I just said, "You did not need to come." But this was not the pattern for all. My own daughter did not want it and profited by choosing instead a private coeducational church-related college (though she did find her future husband in her one-year stay at a land-grant college).

On us in the large state institutions is placed the responsibility for satisfying the needs of our people for the varied educational opportunities required for a nation of 170 million people—who, for better or worse, believe that their children and their country are helped by these opportunities. We must provide the medical schools and the engineering schools, the home economics colleges, and—yes—the arts colleges for those who don't want a Methodist girls' college in Virginia or a Lutheran coeducational university in Tacoma.

KEEP ROLE IN FOCUS

But you have the chance, by your size and your tradition, to keep in sharp focus the traditional role of the college: to preserve in the curriculum and to disseminate the essential principles of our Christian civilization; to develop and strengthen an informed leadership, basically grounded in those essentials of the humanistic tradition; to inculcate in your student group the principles of high ethical and spiritual living. You have the chance to do these very directly.

You have a group which has chosen to come to you to secure these, among other things. *We* must develop a Christian concern through the individual teacher, rather than through the institutional program. *You* can well be the

11

balance wheel—or can balance the programs of the state institutions in these areas.

Some proponents of the utilitarian have failed to comprehend the fundamental nature of the general training for life. That phase of thought, prevalent in my college days, is passing. More and more we see a growth of understanding and mutual respect, a realization of the need for interdependency in educational services.

This country will continue to need the trade school, the technical school, and, of course, the great professional schools of law, theology, medicine, and engineering, with their immediate emphasis on the techniques and skills of a particular job, business, or profession. But along with all this and basic to it all, we need the college in its original simplicity, concentrating on what is its major job, its greatest contribution to the welfare of society—in training young men and young women in the art of thinking. And, I hasten to say, not thinking in a vacuum, but thinking in and about the fundamental laws and operations of a good society, of a good and abundant and rewarding life. Thinking to prepare themselves for leadership, thinking in order to enjoy life more fully, thinking in order to develop their powers better, thinking in order to serve in the highest measure in every phase of human life.

Hence, I have no doubt that Pacific Lutheran and WSU stand, not as rivals, but shoulder to shoulder as partners in a task that will try the resources of both of us in the years ahead.

To my partner, therefore, I say, "God-speed."

DR. LEWIS B. PERRY
President, Whitman College

DR. PERRY gave this address at the homecoming banquet for Pacific Lutheran University alumni on October 15, 1960.

To What End?

IT IS AN HONOR FOR ME to have the privilege of participating in this program that is of such import to you. I also am pleased to be with your able president. The strides made by Pacific Lutheran under his leadership are well known and bid fair to become even greater in the future. Under him, your University has not only retained but increased its distinctly Christian emphasis, influence and outlook. The institution we are honoring tonight feels a deep concern for the moral and religious welfare of its students partly because it reflects Seth Eastvold's concern.

Your president introduced me as an economist, among other things. He took a chance when he asked me to speak with that kind of a background. I need only remind you that Lincoln's Gettysburg Address contains 266 words. The Ten Commandments in the King James edition contain 197 words. The Declaration of Independence contains 300 words. And the OPS order to reduce the price of cabbage, written by an economist, contains 26,911 words. It appears that if you know what you are saying it can be said briefly —if not, it takes more work to create the proper confusion. Hence you ask me to speak at your own risk. I hope you are not as confused at the end of my talk as was the woman who tried to follow a tip passed on by a home economist in a newspaper article when she was alleged to have said that "Lettuce won't turn brown if you put your head in a plastic bag before placing it in a refrigerator."

STUDENT MOTIVATION

One of the most baffling questions facing higher education, and parenthetically, secondary schools today is that of student motivation. It is not one of easy off-hand solution. Various devices are being, and have been, used in an attempt to get students to do their best with the educational opportunities that are available. These include honor programs, independent study projects, undergraduate theses, free in contrast to reserve book shelves, directed studies in various fields, advanced placement, and other devices singly or in combination with one another.

Many approaches to motivation seem to assume that there is something wrong with the student—that for some unknown reason students study and read few books in college and even fewer after they graduate because there is something intrinsically missing within them. Is this the reason why young men and women come to college better able to read and study than ever before yet do little beyond unavoidable assignments and hardly read anything at all other than newspapers after they get a degree? I must argue that I do not believe this is so. Rather, I think the difficulty we face in this area is not easy to solve because it is a result of a combination of forces.

One of these is certainly the popular culture in which we live on and off the campus. The magazines of widest circulation are of a picture nature, similar to the books I read to my six-year-old. The assumption is that the average adult has an attention span equivalent to that of a first grader—unfortunately the assumption may all too often be correct. Television now peers like an all-seeing eye into most of our living rooms. It can be used for stimulating purposes but it is more often than not far from that—to entertain, to persuade the consumer, to act as an escape from reality—but certainly not often to educate or enlighten. I must admit, however, that it does have virtues for harassed mothers at 5:30 p.m. when the kids are about their feet while they are seeking to get supper on the table.

Modern culture is certainly designed to appeal to the eye and the other organs of sense. It has developed to the point where even men's underwear can now be bought for color and fabric design. Think of the satisfaction one gets in knowing that one's under shorts are in the latest color and pattern. Sometimes this satisfaction is more obvious as in the case of the student in the southern California college who went to the library, calmly took off his pants revealing his lovely red shorts, and pressed his trousers with an iron brought along for the occasion.

But a part of this culture intrudes on the campus. In late summer ads in newspapers point out that one will simply get nowhere on campus unless one is dressed in what fashion has decreed is *the latest*. Fraternity rushing interferes with the more serious business of trying to find out what college is basically all about. Social organizations cause students often to consider the week as a rather distasteful interlude between lovely week ends. Some students who are not chosen for particular organizations get their values so warped that they leave school or transfer, mistaking the chaff for the wheat. Intercollegiate athletics becomes an end in itself and the college only a stage. But the diversions are not all of this nature for an intellectual climate also can be watered down by excessive vocationalism or professionalism in an undergraduate institution. The curriculum thus becomes cluttered with "how-to-do-it" courses rather than "how-to-think" offerings.

TEACHING METHODS

A second factor that hampers student motivation too frequently is the teaching methods used by faculty members. It should be granted at this point that much is being undertaken these days to experiment with new teaching methods. The Carnegie Foundation for the Advancement of Teaching has worked in this area for years and is still hard at it. Many of the programs aimed at encouraging the superior student have a laudatory sideline purpose of improving the techniques of getting material across to *all* students. The best teachers never reach perfection in their own minds and are never beyond a willingness to experiment with more effective methods of presentation.

Yet faculty people themselves are still to blame for some lack of motivation on the part of students. I refer, for example, to the man who reads his lectures from textbooks, the individual who uses the blackboard as though he were the only one looking at it, the teacher who puts books on reserve under a schedule that really prevents effective use. And then there is the professor who dotes on volume reading assignments without reference to significance. He is, perhaps to be tolerated more than the professor who consistently insulates himself so as to spend as little time as possible with students in order to follow personal pleasures and goals—he is likely to muse that "college teaching would be wonderful if it weren't for the students." There also is the faculty man who uses teaching methods in the freshman year that kill whatever natural desire for learning his students bring from high school, refusing to believe that students can learn on their own outside the classroom. We as faculty people are never likely to produce students work-

16

ing near their capacity or graduates who will continue this pattern as long as we are *primarily* interested in research, community projects, or committee assignments over and above the kind of effective teaching which encourages the learning process.

HERITAGE REJECTION

A further but not necessarily final factor hampering student motivation is the present college generation's too frequent rejection of the heritage the older generation tries to pass on to it. Perhaps in my college generation this was characterized by the phrase "so what?" Today it is epitomized by the shallow, faithless, and often false thinking behind words and phrases relating to "total destruction," "the edge of the abyss," and "existentialism." It is here that a college can mean so much or so little. Joseph Sittler of the Federated Theological Faculty of the University of Chicago spoke of this when he addressed the second combined plan conference on engineering and the liberal arts under the auspices of Columbia University at Arden House in October, 1957:

> To pull us into the whirlpool of that central passion of the human race is what a college is for! A college ought to be a place where one gravely weighs the invitation to join the human race. A college exists to violate intellectual innocence. We are all in a situation that *always,* sometimes quietly, sometimes traumatically, batters us in a dizzy process of construction, demolition, new construction. We think we understand, and are pounded by facts which demolish our understanding—then build again a deeper and broader-based formulation.

He then went on to say:

> The glory of this human drama is utterly missed if we suppose that men will be content to settle for tolerable order, or merely provisional meaning! We want true and significant order, meaningful patterns, embellishments. We want things to have such a structure that they evoke and affirm man's subterranean convic-

17

tion that the entire gaudy enterprise is not a tale told by an idiot, signifying nothing. Life means——means terribly.

We can only see this meaning if we know the past with its joys and its sorrows, its struggles and its liberations, its mysteries and its clarities. How can one reject the past when he does not know it? One cannot even be a demolition expert unless there is something to demolish! It is a function of a college or university to liberate. This is certainly a truism. But this liberation is not from the old captivities, confusion, naiveté, superstition, the mystery of existence and death, the burden of self-consciousness. Nor is this liberation to make students happy, contented, secure or even indifferent. Its function is rather to liberate a student from individual life into involvement in this human heritage. Looking into the abyss is not the same as jumping into it. Look back into the past for there may be something that will enable the human race to cross the abyss—not fall into it. "So what?" begs the question if we are not willing to accept some of the answers based on the past. Student motivation in an educational institution can never be oriented toward intellectual advancement if those with answers to the question of despair or cynicism, which are based on the best of man's heritage, are ignored

So far I have been talking about student motivation—and particularly about obstacles to doing one's best. Little has been said about the question of this talk "To What End?" which is, in the final analysis, the *sine qua non* on the motivation issue. The "what" likewise has many facets but basically refers to the question of purpose. A century and a quarter ago a young French nobleman, De Tocqueville, returned home and wrote a study of his impressions called *Democracy in America*. In my opinion, every United States citizen should read it. Get a copy if you don't know it. It is in a paperback edition. De Tocqueville saw in the early 1830's the rise of two world powers, Russia and the United

States, and stated that each nation was slated to " . . . hold in its hands the destinies of half the world." What is troublesome to us today is to read De Tocqueville and recognize that he was at that time raising an issue which is extremely significant for us in the new decade. In trying to ascertain how the United States would meet its destiny he sought but did not find the answer to the question of why there are " . . . so many ambitious men and so little lofty ambition found in the United States." "To What End?" To the end that what motivates us to do our best in academic pursuits may also carry over into after life and enable us to participate effectively in this destiny dedicated to lofty ambitions.

Nearly thirty years ago José Ortega y Gasset delivered a series of lectures that were later published under the title *Mission of the University*. If you will read it you will find it among other things to be a strong and still valid criticism of higher learning. But there is one word in the first lecture that best translates into "slovenliness." In Ortega's opinion, slovenliness is the principal illness of governments, universities, students, and people in general. He goes on to state that the opposite of slovenliness is *to be in form*. Here he uses the example of the athlete who is in form and compares him to the significantly different situation when he is out of form. In Ortega's judgment, individuals, groups and countries "out of form" fail. By achieving academic distinction we are demonstrating that we are getting in form, that we are not slovenly, that perhaps we may be working toward lofty ambition. However, the college or university must do more than restate conventional wisdom. There must be purpose in what it offers. It must constantly define and redefine its aims, goals, and objectives—an extremely difficult yet extremely necessary process. In other words, it must also be in form.

Heavier responsibilities

There is another way of looking at this question of "To What End?" that we hear much of the time, yet may be inclined to ignore as a truism. Basically, what students will be able to carry in terms of a heavy or light load of responsibility in later years in society is going to depend to a great degree on what they do with themselves during their university days. Are they going to be fully equipped to furnish their nation with the leadership it is going to need in what may be extremely troubled years in their lives? There is little question but that the demands that will be placed on the backs of today's student generation will be greater than those met by its parents. Trusted and authoritative scientists tell us that each passing day faces us with a responsibility that is growing more serious, namely, the challenge of international communism. Communism as an ideological concept has turned out to be a problem to the free world, but backed by the full power and force of Soviet science it can be catastrophic in its implication if we fail.

We can try to ignore the shock of the past two years and more of seeing Russia make great scientific advances, but we cannot overlook its implications of a need for more emphasis on education and quality achievement in this country. The Soviets have looked on education as a weapon and their investment in it has been proportionally much greater than ours. We have put one-third as much into educating our children in a given year as we have in drinking, smoking and recreation. We love the variety in our educational system; we do not like the monolithic structure of the Soviets, but we cannot question their seriousness of purpose. The latter has been obvious to nearly all American observers. Soviet teachers, researchers, and students all seem to believe that in education there is prestige and a good life, hence there is an internal desire to acquire knowledge whether for financial reward or life satisfaction. "To What End?" Here is a part of the *what* even though it may not be a particular student's reason for his achievement. And this is not new. In 1916, Alfred North Whitehead, one of America's greatest all-time scholars, a man who was perhaps best known as a philosopher, said:

In the conditions of modern life the rule is absolute: The race which does not value trained intelligence is doomed. Not all your heroism, not all your social charm, not all your wit, not all your victories on land or at sea, can move back the finger of fate. Today we maintain ourselves. Tomorrow science will have moved forward yet one more step, and there will be no appeal from the judgment which will then be pronounced on the uneducated.[1]

In September, 1959, Dr. J. R. Goldstein, vice president and director of the RAND Corporation, pointed toward this question of why we should be concerned with academic achievement when he spoke of referring this issue to one of his distinguished colleagues. As Dr. Goldstein stated it, his colleague thought for some time and then spoke as if every word were an effort: "I guess I think that if they work like dogs and if they're lucky, they'll have a chance to participate in history. I guess I think if both these things don't happen it is likely their history will be finished before they are."[2] Gloomy? Perhaps. But even old Ben Franklin was concerned with the question in a more optimistic way when he stated that "The good education of youth has been esteemed by wise men of all ages as the surest foundation of the happiness both of private families and of commonwealths."

A student may, of course, be of a different stripe in this matter of the achievement of academic distinction or quality. He can look on doing his best in his studies during his university career because of sheer financial greed and desire for social status although, God forbid, I hope that it is not behind the achievement of many students today. The American Council on Education pointed out several years ago that a well-recommended Bachelor of Arts degree from a good college or university amounts to additional earning power over a lifetime of $100,000 to $125,000 for the recip-

---

[1]Financing Higher Education 1960-70 (New York: McGraw-Hill, 1959) p. 9.
[2]Address to Harvey Mudd College, "Will We Deserve Our Inheritance?", September 22, 1959.

21

ient over the person who has not received same. These dollar figures, of course, say nothing about the other values that we hope would accrue to the person who had put forth his or her best in taking advantage of the opportunities opened up during four years—perhaps one of the last times when one has a chance to read widely, selectively and with more leisure, in spite of what are considered pressures, until retirement forty-five years later.

RISE ABOVE MEDIOCRITY

The last thing I want to say, in speaking of the desire to rise above the mediocre in academic pursuits, still points to the question "To What End?" In a sense it takes off from the gloomy statement by Dr. Goldstein's friend, for it refers to tomorrow's leadership. During the past dozen years I have been primarily an economist. My work has placed me in contact with a great many business, educational, religious and governmental leaders, both local and national. One element the greatest among them more often than not have had in common has been the fact that they have been generalists. This does not mean that they were never specialists or technicians. It does mean that somewhere along the line they recognized the need to see beyond the horizons of their own discipline. Practicality was not enough. Specialization was not enough. In a fiercely competitive world the narrowness of viewpoint and shallowness of interest which can come from too much specialization and vocationalism can keep a man or woman from reaching the heights of leadership where he or she can be of more effective use in serving mankind. This leadership is a quality we need desperately today and will need even more tomorrow. Too many leaders or would-be leaders today are handicapped by their failure to have the vision that can come from excellence in a field of broadening interest. Their handicap leads to fright and fright to mere expedients—a matter of "after me the deluge." With this attitude on the part of too many leaders, the led get skeptical even though they may get better off materially. Everywhere they feel an emptiness at society's core and seek a new focus to lend form, purpose, and order to life. From where is it to come?

It can come from students at a Christian university represented by Pacific Lutheran. Its curriculum is being based on a broad foundation. It has shown that it can rise above mediocrity. To what end? Toward the removal of the emptiness at society's core and the provision of a new focus to lend form, purpose, and order to the lives of many.

Pacific Lutheran is your university. It is more than a group of Christian scholars working for a common purpose —it is a Christian academic community seeking to answer the question "To What End?" You can help it continue to provide a better answer by your gifts, your prayers, and by sending your children. The result? "Your sons and your daughters shall prophesy, your old men shall dream dreams, your young men shall see visions" (Joel 2:28).

DR. J. C. K. PREUS
*Executive Secretary, Department of Christian Education,
The Evangelical Lutheran Church, 1931-56*

DR. PREUS gave this lecture for the unveiling of memorial plaques in the Tacoma-Pierce Administration Building on October 15, 1961.

The Palace of Truth

A SERIES OF MEMORIALS, including this chapel, are today being unveiled and dedicated. Behind each one of them there lies a story—a story of love, of admiration, and gratitude, perhaps of sorrow, but also of rejoicing.

As the names of those to be memorialized are recalled, there will pass before the mind's eye of some of us the life, the labors, the kindnesses of some beloved person. In our hearts we will thank our heavenly Father for these honored men and women who have gone before, for the precious memories they have left us, for the comfort and inspiration their lives have brought us, for the worthy example each one has set before us.

Whether the memorial gift is great or small—in whatever form it appears—it is an expression of that loyalty and devotion which is essential to the building and development of institutions such as this University.

These memorials are an expression of the understanding of the essential importance of Christian education; they are an appreciation of what this institution has done for some individual or family, for a community or for the church in this territory; they are in a sense a tribute to the efforts of the many men and women who built this institution, who struggled through great difficulties to maintain it, who with indomitable courage continued to labor and sacrifice even when faced with almost insuperable obstacles. Surely these memorials will be a lasting encouragement to others in this and coming generations.

May I at this point dwell for a few moments on the possible significance of the magnificent gift of the late Mr. Jacob Samuelson and his family. This chapel, which will bear the Samuelson name, could come to occupy a place of very special meaning in the life of this University, its faculty and students.

Not long ago the Royal Bank of Canada distributed an article entitled *Education for Democracy*. In the article was this rather interesting statement: "The Palace of Truth is four square, with a gate on every side, so that people may reach it from opposite sides of the compass."

The Christian college or university may in a very special sense be called the Palace of Truth. For it is in very fact the center of a great universal effort to find and understand the truth; and the search is being pressed from every side and every angle. The gates are open for any and every approach.

GATES OF ENTRY

There is the gate of philosophy through which man through the ages has sought to enter the *Palace of Truth*. The deep thinkers of the ages have persistently sought the truth—by reason, by logic, by speculation and analysis. By their efforts many truths have been clarified and established.

Another gate to the Palace of Truth is found in the scientific approach. This gate has been sprung wide open in our age. The telescope, the microscope, the test tube are constantly revealing new secrets in nature. Electronics, the atoms, outer space—terms which in their development and end results stagger the imagination. Science has, indeed barged into the Palace of Truth.

From another "point of the compass" we have the theological approach to truth. Here are the constantly on-going studies and searchings into the deep recesses of revealed truth. Here we have the eternal, changeless truths by which man lives: the truth about God, the great I Am; about Jesus Christ who alone can say "I am the Truth"—about man, sin, salvation, and life eternal.

And speaking of gates to the Palace of Truth we think also of the approach through history and literature with all they tell us of the wisdom and folly, the struggles, failures and successes of man through the ages. We think of psychology and psychiatry with their probing into the nature of man: his mind and soul.

With all this searching, delving, probing into the various realms of truth there must also go insight, understanding. In a broad sense this will be achieved when there is integration or synthesis of all the various elements of truth discovered in the Palace of Truth.

In their efforts to find this understanding, students and teachers alike may find this peaceful chapel, the Jacob Samuelson Chapel, to be significantly helpful. To think, to analyze, to evaluate, a person should be able to withdraw to a place of undisturbed silence. There, if anywhere, a person should be able to examine his relationship to God and to his fellow men. There it may be possible for him to reappraise his work and his faith, discover what he holds to be absolute truth and what is only relative. There, also, he may be able in his thinking to bring into proper relationship all that he has discovered in the Palace of Truth.

To one who teaches others, such periods of self examination and self appraisal are all-important. There is always the possibility and danger that a person may teach a course, any course, without giving thought to its possible relationship to other subjects a student may be studying.

Various sciences may indeed be taught and studied without reference to philosophy and theology, but if so they will be without that deeper meaning which all of God's marvelous creations should have for the Christian. To teach theology and philosophy without relating them in any way to the wonders and achievements of science, is to fail to give to God the glory and honor which nature in all its realms accords the almighty and all-wise Creator of heaven and earth.

In this turbulent period of history there is desperate need for time, undisturbed time, to ponder deeply what and how we teach the younger generation and to evaluate carefully the influence of our personal lives upon the character and development of our students.

This chapel extends to teacher and student alike a warm invitation to withdraw from the restless activities of the campus, for periods, or even moments, of silent undisturbed meditation. A detached and prayerful look at one's life and labors, one's motives and aspirations, will be intellectually refreshing and spiritually cleansing.

Not long ago the Prime Minister of Burma visited Washington. As is customary with foreign dignitaries, he was "put up" at the Blair house, the President's guest house. During his stay a third floor room was set apart and sanctified for his private use. Every morning the Prime Minister rose at five o'clock and repaired to this room for undisturbed meditation and worship before an improvised Buddhist altar.

May the facilities afforded by the Jacob Samuelson Chapel stimulate in members of the University family a compelling desire to cultivate the practice of undisturbed meditation and worship before the altar of our only Lord Jesus Christ.

DR. HAROLD L. YOCHUM
President, Capital University

DR. YOCHUM gave this lecture when he dedicated
the Memorial Stone to Great Teachers in front of
the new administration building on December 7,
1960.

The Habitual Vision of Greatness

IN THESE DAYS OF THE unsanforized dollar, it may seem as
though higher education deserves that designation in terms
of its financial cost, if in no other respect. The old joke is
pertinent as well as pert: "college bred" means a "four-year
loaf on father's dough." I would add that this takes a lot of
crust! While the cost is high in terms of time and money,
a college education is still one of today's best bargains. Actually, the fees charged students at Pacific Lutheran or
Capital or most of our good colleges have not increased as
much as rising costs of education and the devaluation of the
dollar would justify. No student pays more than about two-
thirds of the actual costs of his college education, even when
he has paid his bill in full. The difference is made up by
church subsidies, endowment income, gifts from alumni

and other friends. We believe that the money spent on your education is a sound investment that will pay rich dividends in the service and leadership which you will provide in your future years. Your higher education is worth all the cost . . . *if* you really get a higher education. It is no secret that some persons can spend four years in college and even graduate without getting a higher education.

It is quite difficult to define education, especially higher education, though you can usually recognize an educated person when you meet one. Surely a higher education worthy of the name must do more than just prepare a person for a chosen profession or job. One of the most disheartening experiences of the educator is to observe that so many students are not really seeking an education—just trying to qualify for a coveted position and its more coveted remuneration. Yes, let us admit, Mr. President, that this happens also in our church colleges with their liberal arts tradition!

Surely, our many hours of study and class attendance, laboratory work and research, must mean more than just meeting requirements for a diploma to meet requirements for a job. So many students work their way through college: some by working their parents, some by working their wives, some by working their professors! But did you get the higher education you were working for? That is the crucial question.

LIBERAL ARTS VERSUS VOCATIONAL TRAINING

Now, do not put me down as a long-haired devotee of liberal arts who disparages vocational or professional training. One who is educated must not only be good, but also good for something. Increasingly, leaders in various professions have recognized that cultural or liberal arts courses should constitute a *larger* part of the prescribed curriculum for future engineers, doctors and those in other professional fields. Here I should like to use a word coined by Father

29

Divine when he said that preachers and professors are awfully smart people, but they just don't know how to tangibilitate. With all our culture and learning we do need to tangibilitate, or put into effective use and practical application what has been offered to us in our program of higher education. In evaluating liberal arts vs. professional courses, we might well heed a popular TV slogan: "Don't settle for one without the other!"

Certainly, an education worthy of the name should increase our proficiency in the various media of communication, the ability to read and listen intelligently and critically, the ability to speak and write intelligibly and effectively. The two-way skill in communication is a vital factor in one's relationships with others and in one's vocation. Words, like pictures, are symbols of ideas, and you cannot always draw pictures for people to get across your ideas.

Certainly, an education worthy of the name should impart some degree of culture, appreciation of music and poetry and painting, all the treasures of former civilizations which are made so readily available to us today if we will but take them. This is not something for only the wealthy or the aged to enjoy—now is the time for you to appreciate and enjoy all the cultural masterpieces of man's creativity.

Certainly, an education worthy of the name should inspire us to sound thinking, sensible decisions, sane self-control. Certainly, an education worthy of the name should broaden our horizons of interest and understanding, deepen our convictions and commitments, uplift our standards and ideals, extend our vision back into all the recorded experiences and achievements of man in the past, forward into the almost limitless possibilities of the future.

All this, and much more, I would read into a phrase which the famous educator, Alfred North Whitehead, used when he wrote that, whatever else education is or does, it should provide "the habitual vision of greatness." How distressing it is to note the prevalence of small men in big places, of small-thinking about big problems, of narrow and short-sighted policies in the face of far-reaching implications and consequences! The interracial and international tensions, juvenile delinquency, and parental delinquency, low moral standards and behavior of so many men and women, which fill up our newspapers every day, indicate how imperative it is that we catch and cultivate the habitual vision of greatness.

INCUBATE GREATNESS

Our educational institutions, whatever else they do, must incubate greatness, must send forth men and women whose character, motivation, outlook on life and impact on their associates will be marked by the indefinable but unmistakable quality of greatness. Somehow along without peering into test tubes and microscopes, or poring over pages of words and columns of figures, we must find adequate time and effective ways to share with one another the habitual vision of greatness. In my opinion, the biggest problem and challenge confronting our educational institutions today— far more important than maintaining academic standards and balancing budgets while providing staff and facilities for the impending deluge of students—is to impart to every one of our students in every department and every activity the habitual vision of greatness.

PURPOSE OF LIFE

You see, we have become so preoccupied with the trivial facts and figures of all our courses, all the what and when and where and how many questions, that we do not always get on to the really basic and important questions, the why and so what questions. We focus our attention on the machinery and phenomena of this physical world and our existence in it, and fail to give sufficient thought to the meaning and purpose of our lives. We are like the driver of an automobile who has checked his motor and gas tank, even weather forecasts, but has no clear notion of where he is going or why he is going anywhere.

This is the point made by Sir Richard Livingstone, president of Corpus Christi College at Oxford, when he said: "we do not know our own minds about the most important things of life. . . . Having no philosophy of life, we drift along, or rather, we slither!" He used the right word for so many: slither. How aptly that describes the course of millions of people through their daily life! No sense of direction, no drive to reach high objectives, just a senseless drifting along, slithering along! What a tragedy!

"The dignity of man," writes Reinhold Niebuhr, "is his freedom, his capacity to make and remake history, to search out all things and to inquire after the meaning of existence." Can it be that when man has mastered the forces of natures as never before, he becomes a slave to his own tools and gadgets? The real threat of automation is not so much to employment or income as to meaningful activity, the maintenance of intellectual vitality during hours of mechanical operations, to the constructive use of increasing hours and days of leisure, to the freedom and dignity of the person, his opportunity for self-expression and self-realization. Can it be that when man is able to measure and analyze and synthesize material things of the universe as never before, he has less understanding of the spiritual things which give life meaning and value? If so, it matters little what grades students make in school, when they flunk the final examination of life itself!

Much the same point is made by Dr. Howard Lowry, president of Wooster College, in his fascinating book, "The Mind's Adventure" as he declares that "life and education are, or should be, the pursuit of significance . . . what makes us live is whatever enhances our capacity to confer a meaning on what we know and feel. . . . But this quest requires a scale of high values and the highest faith possible to man." He adds, "Secularism has not furnished an adequate sense of these values or an adequate drive toward them."

So we see ourselves as more than laboratory specimens of biochemistry and mechanics, or puppets of fate and chance. We have a dignity, a freedom, a responsibility as human beings so that we can maintain our convictions in the face of intimidation, our integrity in the face of temptation, our ideals in the face of frustration.

It is that element of true greatness which is so urgently needed in men and women everywhere today, and which it is the high privilege of colleges to give to their students. You cannot be satisfied with the lesser values of life, with mediocrity, with being "Mr. Average." You know that persons are more important than things, that moral and spiritual realities mean more than material realities, that you are called upon to make a life and not just a living, that you have a destiny to fulfill which shall be written on the record for all eternity.

> To every man there openeth
>   a way and ways, and a way;
> The high soul climbs the high way
>   and the low soul gropes the low,
> While in between, on the misty flats
>   the rest drift to and fro;
> But to every man there openeth
>   a high way and a low
> And every man decideth
>   which way his soul shall go.

That third dimension, the dimension of altitude, is the distinctive factor in greatness, and any vision of greatness. One must rise above the horizontal dimensions of life to achieve greatness. Longevity of life as such is no virtue, nor even breadth of experience and understanding. It takes the upward tug of God at our hearts and lives to invest them with greatness.

With William Cullen Bryant, we gaze at the solitary waterfowl as it wings its way toward its destination, and we whisper:

He who from zone to zone
　　Guides through the boundless sky thy certain flight,
In the long way that I must tread alone
　　Will lead my steps aright.

With Sidney Lanier we stare out over the wide spaces of the marshes of Glynn, and we murmur:

"As the marsh-hen secretly builds on the watery sod, Behold, I will build me a nest on the greatness of God. I will fly in the greatness of God as the marsh-hen flies, In the freedom that fills all the space 'twixt the marsh and the skies. By so many roots as the marsh grass sends in the sod, I will heartily lay me a hold on the greatness of God."

RELIGION IN HIGHER EDUCATION

It is this awareness of the reality and relevance of God and the things of the spirit that characterize the vision of greatness and lifts us above the low and sordid things of life. There *is* a place for the teaching of true religion in higher education! We may become so preoccupied with gadgets and gimmicks that we ignore goodness and God. Robert Hutchins, while president of the University of Chicago, declared, "If a college or university is going to think about important things, then it must think about religion." And Sir Richard Livingstone flatly said, "Anyone in western civilization who has not thought seriously about Christianity is not really educated." Church and colleges like Pacific Lutheran and Capital can and must be avowedly and unashamedly Christian in our framework of reference for teaching and in all our activities and policies.

Precisely because we have evaded or ignored the moral and spiritual issues of life and neglected the religious education of our young people we have become what Elton Trueblood so graphically calls a "cutflower civilization." The roots of our culture go down deep into our religious beliefs and heritage—but so many of this generation have been cut off from those roots. No wonder they feel a lack of assurance, of security, find no meaning in life, despair of any valid norm of truth and goodness, seek satisfaction in superficial and sensate pleasures! People cannot starve their souls, deny or defy God, violate all the conditions of successful living and then expect to enjoy successful lives! Like former civilizations, we can go on for a time by virtue of the heritage of previous generations, utilizing the spiritual energy stored up in the cut-off stems, but soon such a culture withers and dies. This is more fatal to the future of America than being surpassed by some other nation in technology or military might.

NOT TAUGHT BUT CAUGHT

When you look back over your experiences on this campus, your class lectures and laboratory experiments, your reading and research, your participation in campus activities, that which means the most to you, that which you will remember when other things are largely forgotten, is the sort of thing I am talking about today. It may be some incidental comment by a professor which escaped from the minutiae of his subject matter and for a moment touched sublime, eternal truth and realities. It may be some remark of a student in a bull-session. It may be some significant experience on a football field or a basketball floor, or even a tender conversation with a sweetheart on a moonlit campus. It may be the groan or sigh of your spirit in some inarticulate prayer to God when you could not sleep at night. It is something that cannot be taught but must be caught; that cannot be reasoned but must be felt; that defies rationalization or adequate verbalization but influences the entire course of your life. It cannot be forced or manufactured, but when it happens, you know that it is of the utmost importance to you and all the years that lie ahead. And let me assure you that there is no more rewarding experience for the teacher or counselor than to feel that he has lifted the veil and given to a receptive student some glimpse of greatness that will stay with him for years. You have the right to expect that kind of teaching at a church college like this, that will impart this habitual vision of greatness. And if you do not at this moment feel that you received it, perhaps wishing that you might have another year or two to get what I have been talking about, let me assure you that the thoughtful person will in later life have experiences which bring to his remembrance many precious words he heard long since and thought he had forgotten.

Perhaps what I have been trying to say to you today can be summarized and symbolized by reference to the famous Pestalozzi statue in Zurich. The citizens of the city wished to honor the great educator by erecting a suitable statue to his memory. So a good artist and sculptor was selected and given the commission. After careful thought, he decided on an appropriate composition: gathered around Pestalozzi were the figures of children gazing with respect and affection into the face of their beloved teacher. That was good, but not good enough. He elevated the gaze of the pupils so that they were looking not at Pestalozzi, but above and beyond him at something and Someone higher. That is the highest tribute anyone could bring to the truly great teacher: that he has directed the minds and hearts of his pupils to something and Someone higher.

Our best wish for you today is that your eyes and lives may have that upward look, blessed and ennobled by the habitual vision of greatness.

Seek first the kingdom of God and his righteousness, and all these things will be added to you. (Matthew 6:33.)

"Set your hearts on his kingdom and his goodness, and all these things will come to you as a matter of course." (Phillips translation.)

DR. ROBERT A. L. MORTVEDT
Executive Director, Board of Christian Higher Education,
The Augustana Lutheran Church and
The United Lutheran Church in America

DR. MORTVEDT gave this lecture on a day set aside for consideration of the humanities on January 18, 1961.

"Poised to Walk on a Star"

I DEEPLY APPRECIATE the friendly welcome which has been accorded me by President Eastvold and his associates, as I come to participate with you in a series of events celebrating your University Year. Having known your president for many years, I am aware of his many accomplishments; and I am proud of his contributions to Lutheran higher education. Under his direction, Pacific Lutheran University has become a strong and respected institution, representing excellence in education *per se,* and exemplifying to a significant degree what it means to be an educational institution of the Lutheran Church.

It gives me pleasure to bring greetings to this entire academic community from the two boards of Christian higher education which I represent, that of the Augustana Lu-

37

theran Church and that of the United Lutheran Church in America. In a very real sense, I bring you the felicitations of twenty colleges and eleven seminaries scattered across the land. Each of them wishes you well as you seek to increase your service to church and nation.

President Eastvold has asked me to give particular attention to the humanities in my address, obviously out of deference to my personal involvement in the field of literature. I am happy to comply, since I believe the study of literature, music, philosophy, religion and languages—both classic and modern—can contribute enormously to solving the problems of the modern world. I would go so far as to say that without profound and continuing studies in these fields, there will be no resolution of our contemporary predicament. In the humanities we must find one, at least, of the essential keys to unlock the doors of the prison of disillusionment or despair in which so many people find themselves today.

To make any reference to the humanities meaningful, it is essential to refer to science; for science is almost the one thing which is reasonably familiar to everyone today. A cartoonist recently depicted the situation vividly by having a very small youngster say to his mother, "Phooey on Little Red Riding Hood! What's the newest thing in solid fuel propellants?" Something of the magnitude of the influence of science in the modern world is revealed by the fact that 90% of the scientists who have *ever* lived are living and working right now!

All of us, I am sure, were impressed by *Time*'s gesture a few weeks ago when it selected a composite of fifteen American scientists as its "man of the year." The record of their achievements is utterly amazing, and I doff my hat with profound respect and admiration.

No salvation in science

One of the fifteen, Chemist Willard Libby, is quoted in the covering article as follows: "We scientists are the only people who are not bored, the only adventurers of modern times, the real explorers—the fortunate ones." In the light of their accomplishments, it is easy to see the basis for such a statement; but I have no hesitation in declaring that I disagree. If what Dr. Libby says is true, we are, indeed, on a very perilous road, and all of us must become deeply concerned. The quoted statement ought to be a stern challenge in any kind of academic community, but it ought to cut to the very heart of concern on the campus of a college or university vitally connected with the Christian Church. To admit that Dr. Libby is correct is tantamount to admitting that the modern world will find its salvation in science, a conclusion which, despite my admiration for the achievements of science, I cannot accept. The likelihood of destroying the world in consequence of man's scientific potential appears to me to be far greater than the likelihood of saving it.

Utilizing the amazing contributions of science, as well as those of all other disciplines, the only really creative course the world can pursue is, in my judgment, that outlined in the Christian Gospel. The solution to our modern predicament can be stated as succinctly as that.

The essence of this brief chapel address is my belief that the modern world needs a spiritual break-through similar to those occurring in the field of science. In my judgment, this is possible, provided capable leaders will plunge into this area of the world's concern with the same confident enthusiasm and zeal manifested by our modern men of science. More has been learned in the fields of science in the last twenty-five years than in all previous history! No one would dream of saying the same thing about the humanities.

This is not to say that we need a new Messiah—far from it! The supreme event of man's religious experience occurred, we believe, two thousand years ago. Just as Christ met all of his contemporaries at the point of their greatest need at that time, so he can do today. The trouble with all too many of us is that we have lived with the glorious news so long that we take it for granted! It is tarnished and commonplace and our indifference divests it of its power. What we need are new interpreters, men and women whose lives have been so powerfully touched by the Christian Gospel that they will speak in the words of Scientist Libby: "We . . . are the only people who are not bored, the only adventurers of modern times, the real explorers—the fortunate ones." We need a new and profound understanding of the Incarnation and the Resurrection, as well as the divine command "Go ye."

WE NEED TRANSFORMATION

I am deeply conscious of the personal impact of these words. If you and I are to be involved in this supremely important enterprise, it is not enough just to listen and nod our heads in agreement. We must become involved! We must submit ourselves as never before to the transforming power of a book and a message. You know as well as I what that book and that message are!

Not long ago, I read a sentence which caught my imagination as few have done for months or even years. It was this: "Never before in the history of mankind has man stood with one foot in his primitive origins and the other foot poised to walk on a star."

The thought in the sentence was evoked by awareness of the fact that scientists are seriously working toward the day when human beings will travel through space at incredible speeds in rocket-propelled vehicles, arriving at their destinations on other planets in accordance with published time-tables. The sentence was written by John R. Milton, chairman of the English Department at Jamestown College, Jamestown, N. D.

Jamestown, as some of you know, is situated on the midst of the seemingly endless great plains of the north, in an area where, as Dr. Milton puts it, "The earth, and our working of it, keeps us basically primitive in spirit. This means," he continues, "that many of our values (though not all) are more fundamental, less artificial, than some of those values which are associated with sophistication. . . . But we have a problem," he says. "We are caught between the old and the new, between the earth and the sky, between the mysteries and possibilities of the future."

As I read these sentences, I asked myself, Are not all thoughtful people today enmeshed in the same mysteries? Certainly you, as university students, ought to be; for you ought, in your privileged position, to be aware of the fact that, "Psychologically, this is perhaps the most important moment in the entire (intellectual) existence of man. Whole new concepts have opened before us, some of them staggering the imagination; and we haven't even had time yet to get used to our simple and immediate past."

A man like Dr. Milton cannot help being aware of such an anomaly, for he is living in an area which *officially* is not more than 75 years old. I mean by officially that historical records do not go back farther than that. Yet that area in North Dakota is on the edge of "one of the oldest strata of identifiable rock on the face of the earth, over two billion years old." A few hundred miles to the southwest is the vastly interesting burial ground of the primeval dinosaurs, and "not far beyond are the mountains, heaved up by some gigantic cataclysm before the memory of man."

Historically we are children. This continent was discovered less than 500 years ago, and it has been settled in the last 340. Most of us have travelled only a few hundred or a few thousand miles in our lifetime; yet we are suddenly "confronted with the problem of getting acquainted with a *universe* rather than a *world*. And all of the problems man has inherited on earth may well be magnified a thousand times in the sky." No one can possibly know what may be in store for mankind as we push out the bounds of our known environment.

CREATURES OF GOD

Startling and baffling as some of these reflections may at first seem, people with your background and mine must find in them inspiration for the vastly important tasks which confront us. Eventually we must remember who we are and whence we came. We are not helpless victims of chance and circumstance. We do not believe we invented ourselves; we believe we were created by God. More than that, we believe we were created in the "image of God." Just what that phrase in all its majesty and mystery embraces, I do not understand. An image, I know, is not the same as the substance it reflects; we are not God, even though we possess seemingly divine powers. But we are different from all other parts of the created world in that we have minds which can learn almost infinitely and can *know* and *remember*. More than that, we have an unquenchable impulse to know simply for the sake of knowing. This can be said of no other created thing. It is the specific quality of our minds which differentiates us from animals and makes us human beings, and which has brought us to the threshold of the space age.

In view of all this, a rather startling thought has occurred to me: Is it true, in the words of Dr. Milton, that "Never before in the history of mankind has man stood with one foot in his primitive origins and the other foot poised to walk on a star"? Is it not rather true—and is not this what we have forgotten?—that, from the moment of his creation, man has possessed this matchless possibility? Is it not this what was meant when we were told that we are "created in the image of God"? Is not this what was demonstrated when Christ, the Son of God, became incarnate and died so that we might be redeemed? Is not this what was promised when Christ declared that he would go to prepare a place for his disciples? Is not this, symbolically speaking, what is meant by the promise of the Resurrection?

The materialists and humanists have been trying to tell us that we are nothing but clay, that we may erect a temporarily enchanting world, but that eventually we shall pass into oblivion. And a lot of us have almost come to believe them! As Christians, however, we do not accept such a view. Instead, with the Psalmist, we can say:

When I consider thy heavens, the work of thy fingers,
  the moon and the stars, which thou hast ordained;
What is man, that thou art mindful of him? and
  the son of man, that thou visitest him?
For thou hast made him a little lower than the angels,
  and hast crowned him with glory and honor.
Thou madest him to have dominion over the works of thy hands;
  thou hast put all things under his feet.

MAN TRANSCENDS TIME AND SPACE

The most challenging problem each one of us confronts in his lifetime is the problem of answering the question, "Who am I?" Tragically, in attempting to answer this question, millions of people have seen themselves at a point far too low on the ladder of possibilities. It was not humility, however, which put them there. It was more likely either ignorance or, paradoxically, arrogance. On the other hand, it is not pride which entices the Christian to believe that he was created for the destined purpose of transcending the limits of both time and space as a redeemed child of God. In a time when man's matchless accomplishments tend, for many people, only to accentuate the expansion of our physical world, we must, as Christians, strive to see the implications as far as our spiritual lives are concerned. Through faith we have always had our feet poised to walk on a star. Too often, however, we have been earthbound, unwilling or afraid to accept the promise of God for the life of the spirit.

Now that the door of our physical world is opened as never before in the history of man, we must also walk forward boldly as the spiritual children of God. Most of us, perhaps, have never even begun to grasp the glorious promises of God toward those who love and serve him.

It is my confirmed judgment that we shall not find the answers to our most basic yearnings by walking through the expanding doors of science, magnificent as the new vistas are. The business of the scientist as scientist is to learn all that can possibly be learned about the physical universe and all its parts. He will endlessly seek to know how things are put together and of what substances or particles they are made; and his inquiring genius will take him into incredible refinements of knowledge.

But God is not composed of atoms or neutrons or protons or anti-matter. God is spirit and he speaks to the yearning spirits of men through great literature and music and art —through the Bible, through human experience, through the lips of men and women who, acknowledging and glorifying in the scintillating achievements of science, still listen to the still, small persistent voice of the Spirit.

The great challenge before all of us is to find the means whereby we can hear that still, small, persistent voice and make it meaningful in a world where scientific miracles have become commonplace.

DR. T. M. STINNETT
Assistant Executive Secretary for Professional Development and Welfare, National Education Association

This address was given February 6, 1961

The Third Frontier

PETER VIERICK HAS SUGGESTED that "America has had three great frontiers: the first two material, the third cultural."[1]

The first was geographic—settlement of the West, extension of the nation to the Pacific. The second was a gadget-and-gimmick-filled culture, with evertowering aspirations for possession of things and money. The first disappeared about 1890 with the disappearance of free land. The second marches on into the future, but in terms of real human progress there begins to be widespread evidence that it is far from enough. The third, which we now begin to seek in earnest, is the frontier of the mind of man—the developed mind of man. This involves an irrevocable trilogy—man's intellectual, cultural and spiritual development. This is the immeasurable frontier; in a very real sense, it is the last frontier.

---

[1] Peter Vierick, *The Unadjusted Man.* Boston: The Beacon Press, 1956, p. 271.

This search may be the harbinger of a vitally needed new perspective in American life. The time has come to put an end to the glamorizing of inconsequential personalities and puny events. Historically, we Americans have tended to reserve our plaudits for the showy, the superficial; to reserve our adulation for the synthetic characters called celebrities, who have been made so by our incredible incantations before physical deviations, either of action or bodily development.

The future of America and of freedom in the world—if either is to survive—rests with mental phenomena, not physical.

The meaning of the kaleidoscopic events of recent years is that the mind of man has become the potential resource for all our hopes and aspirations as a people. It is faulty divination that judges the future as the age of outer space. It is, in reality, to be the age of inner space—the space between the ears and behind the eyes of men. It is to be the age of the expanding fruits of the developed minds of men.

Man is edging into a totally new era in his history—one so drastically promising as to defy the imagination. It is to be an era in which all the old power structures of the past, by which nations subsisted or predominated, will become obsolete. The successive, evolutionary states of power structures—colonialism, sea power, even of air power, will retreat into limbo or become subservient to the advancing achievements of intellectual power.

And the search for the new power source will become increasingly feverish. When President Truman, in announcing the Hiroshima incident in August of 1945, said: "We stand at the door of destruction or upon the threshold of the greatest age of man," he forecast, perhaps far greater than he knew, changes and potentials in society that threaten to outrace our ability to keep abreast or to comprehend. This event was the declaration of the ending of one era in man's history and the beginning of another. It did not foretell that within a decade there would be several such endings and new beginnings.

46

Perhaps the major frustration we face now is that new ages have impinged upon us with such rapidity in the short space of a decade and a half that we find it impossible to adjust to them quickly enough to grasp, even dimly, their implications. In man's slow progress out of the jungle, the line of demarcation between one epoch and another had always been an imperceptible thread that meandered lazily and erratically through centuries. But at Hiroshima, in an instant, clearly marked for the eyes of all men to see, was the end of one era in history and the beginning of another. Suddenly, as two ships at sea with their binding thongs severed move apart, so at Hiroshima the cleavage between the past and the future was clearly exposed in an instant. And though men saw this with their own eyes, they saw not its meaning.

This is understandable. It took man nearly 400,000 years to emerge from the role of a nomadic hunter and a gleaner of the fruits of nature for his food into agriculture. Only 200 years ago did he bring forth the Industrial Revolution. But since 1945, three new and distinct eras have come to pass—the fission age, the fusion age, and the space age. And these three, as puzzling and indistinct as their full imports yet are, were forerunners of the power shifts of nations, from the patterns of the past to brain power, as the hope for survival of men on earth, as the promise of a still greater horizon for the best aspirations yet ahead.

II.

Why has man's mind become the immeasurable frontier so suddenly, so irrevocably? For at last three reasons—reasons which have emerged together. (1) The incredible population explosion; (2) the accelerated accretion of new knowledge; (3) the upsurge of new nations with new aspirations for freedom and dignity.

One has only to take a superficial look at the unprecedented increase in the modern world of the number of mouths to feed, the number of bodies to clothe and shelter,

47

to realize that the essential nonrenewable resources of nature are disappearing with such alarming rapidity. There is no other way to state the resultant threat except as a race between education and catastrophe, which H. G. Wells predicted almost a half-century ago. And these figures reveal, as nothing else can, that man must create from the frontiers of his own mind the physical necessities of survival which, in the past and in most areas of the world, nature so bountifully supplied.

Consider the awesome facts of the population explosion. In the year One A.D., the world's population was about 250 millions. Sixteen centuries, or until about the time of the founding of America, were required to double this population. In the following 300 years, the world's population quadrupled, to reach about two billions. Within the past 30 years, this has grown to three billions. If the present rate of growth continues, in a half century, by the year 2000 A.D., it will reach six billions; and in a century, nine billions.

The world's population is now growing at the rate of 43 millions a year, adding another United States to the population every four years. Tomorrow morning at this time, there will be in the world 125,000-150,000 additional mouths to feed. In the United States alone, the experts tell us, we shall have reached a population of 250 millions of people by 1980; and a century from now, if the present rate of growth continues, we shall have a population of 600 millions. Some one has recently calculated that the number of people supportable by the earth is 50 billions, 20 times the present population. And that this could be reached in 175 years if the present growth rate remains unchecked.

It would be a crowded world—20 times as crowded as today. It would be a world in which all animal protoplasm would be replaced by human protoplasm. One could not afford the luxury of maintaining dogs or cows or horses or pigs, or even probably, the large creatures in zoos. All edible material would have to go down the throats of hungry people.

As for the second factor—the accretion of new knowledge

—this is the fruit of an intellectual revolution which has been sweeping the world in the last century, in the forefront of which is science. Science has been projected into the lexicon of the educated man, as an essential component of liberal education. The staggering rate of accumulation of new knowledge in this field can best be illustrated perhaps by the recent assertion of a famous scientist that, "One half of all scientists who ever lived are still alive."

As for the third—the upsurge of new nations—this has created a new and puzzling array of problems for us. The problem of freedom in the world is no longer a bi-polar one. It is multiple polar.

III.

These things have profound implications for the education of Americans, indeed of all people.

First, the quality of teaching and learning must be stepped up drastically. Obsolescence alone forces education to shed the emphases of the past upon the inculcation of simple skills and knowledges and increasingly concentrate upon the development of people at professional, scientific, and technical levels. Some two or three years ago, the producers of the giant computer machines predicted that they would require by 1965 something like 175,000 professionals to supervise and direct the functioning of these machines. Thus, within a decade, an entirely new profession, in size almost as large as the medical profession, must be prepared by our colleges and universities.

Professional workers were less than five per cent of our labor force in 1900; by 1975, they will constitute about 15 per cent. Farm workers in 1900 were nearly 4c per cent of our labor force; by 1975, they will represent little more than five per cent. Even today there are 10 million fewer people on the farm than 20 years ago; and they are feeding 50 millions more people, and we are plagued by surpluses. And what about unskilled labor? In 1900 unskilled laborers were 12.5 per cent of the total labor force; in 1975, they will be less than five per cent. The higher level and quality of education in the future are dictated by these facts.

Second, there is the problem of the fruitful uses of time. And just here is where the cultural and spiritual parts of the trilogy come into focus. Soon each American will have one-half of all his time to himself, for his very own to do with as he will. Thus, a persistent dream of man will become a reality. But this fact, *per se,* is not significant. What is significant is the use he will make of this time. If we are enabled to do no more with it than indulging in spectatoritis; in killing each other by the thousands on the highways each weekend in our frantic haste to go nowhere in particular; in passively soaking up TV shows, surfeiting ourselves with slogans and stereotypes, in short, in squandering it in mental, moral and physical vegetation, then this added time will prove to be a curse, not a blessing.

Here is a new frontier for education and, thus, for men's minds. Education for the future must set Americans in search of the instinctive and intuitive upper reaches of the human spirit; in pursuit of added riches for the mind in the sciences, the arts, literature, and music; in pursuit of knowledge and creativeness for their own sakes, as much or more so than for their utilitarian rewards. Only in this way can our society avoid the inexorable inroads of conformity and manipulation. For the arts and creativeness are incurably individualistic.

But can the standards of education be stepped up so radically and so rapidly in a society where work hours grow constantly shorter, where life grows ever softer, where the "pleasure up" slogan of the advertising world is constantly hammered into the public consciousness as a new and appealing religion? Can the high school and college student be impelled to honor and covet intellectual effort and achievement in a climate of disdain, in a climate that seems to exalt animalism?

The answer is that the standards of education and of individual achievement must be stepped up, in the face of these hard realities. The major task of educators is to find the rationale for making respectable, for conferring prestige upon intellectual achievement—to find a rationale for impelling students to still greater efforts in a society that tends always to travel in the other direction. Does society have a right to demand this? It is not a matter of right, it is a matter of no other alternative—except disaster.

I think Dr. James B. Conant's answer to the drive for higher standards of achievement and work for students is sound. He says the way to justify this to students is the concept that, after all, "You are working for yourself." It is not a clock-punching job; it is the pursuit of the best and richest and finest in your own life. And such a pursuit is not measurable in terms of what others do; it can only be measured in terms of the unsearchable riches of the human spirit.

IV.

But this imperative for quality in education cannot, in my judgment, be predicated, as so many now seem to advocate, upon worship of the tough for toughness' sake; upon the authoritarian for discipline's sake; or upon regimentation, for regimentation's sake. It cannot be predicated upon fear, upon threats, or upon breast-beating lamentations of the self-elected critics of whatever is, who abound in some numbers in every community. *It must and can be predicated upon the joy of intellectual adventure, upon the sense of power inherent in creativeness, upon the supreme sense of well-being flowing from achievement over and beyond the call of duty.*

The American people have always done what they had to do. So have our youth, although both have sometimes been tardy in clearly recognizing what had to be done. The college student who finds himself classed among the select group for which we have coined the term "gifted," not only should thank God for his uncommon gifts, but should realize that real gratitude can only be given expression through dedication to the hard work which only can give meaningful substance to such a rare blessing. The ultimate in failure is the negative of one's talents. The ultimate in successful living is to measure up to the full potential of whatever talents with which one is endowed.

In this connection, I must express my dissent from the prevalent and popular notion that real intellectual potentials reside only in the upper 15 or 20 per cent of our student population. Intellectual powers differ among human beings, of course, but intellectual achievement of each normal human being in search of his highest and best can be precious to America and its hopes for the future. And on this thesis, I must assert my vigorous dissent from the increasingly popular notion that this nation should not, and cannot afford the costly venture of providing the opportunity of higher education for more than a select few.

As Josiah Royce once said: "Thinking is like loving and dying; each man must do it for himself." The denial of this thesis is the road to disaster; it is a negation of our past, and an ominous threat to our future.

One cannot but mistrust the current and insistent clamor for rigor in education, based upon competition with the Soviets, or upon the presumed rigor of education of the past, which so many parents in their nostalgic remembrance of their school days always translate into incredible ruggedness.

I find myself strongly drawn to an off-the-cuff statement by Robert Frost, in a recent appearance on "Meet the Press." He said, "I'd rather go down as an Athenian than survive as a Spartan. All this frenzy to toughen up our schools in imitation of Russia is all wrong. I want our schools toned up—but to the Athenian ideal, not the Spartan."

This, the toning up of education in America to the Athenian ideal, it seems to me, is but the concept of the developed mind of man, is the search for America's third frontier, the search for America's immeasurable frontier, perhaps of America's last frontier.

DR. ALVIN N. ROGNESS
President, Luther Theological Seminary

One of a series of sermons given by DR. ROGNESS
during Spiritual Emphasis Week, Feb. 12-16, 1961.

Wanted: A King

LIFE OFTEN BECOMES LIKE A BOUQUET—a cluster of things.
There are health and pleasure and friends and work and
reputations and success. Most people want a big, full bouquet.

People are not agreed on what really is the important
thing. Some people will sell their friends for money, others
give their money to help their friends. Some will defraud
and cheat to be successful, others would give up gain and
prestige before surrendering their honesty.

In the long run some one thing will get you. You have
not but one life to live and finally some one thing will control that life. It may be pleasure. You work, you keep well,
you make friends, you earn money—all in order to find new
pleasures. You bend all of life toward the goal of more and
more pleasure. It may be success. You study and work hard,
you choose the right friends, you guard your health, you

53

amass money—all in order to win in a grim competition with other people. Nothing counts really but to end up at the top of the heap.

ONE RULING DESIRE

Life tends to narrow down to some one, controlling desire. Some ambition, some passion, some desire will become King and rule all others. You have but one life, and with it you can get one prize. King Midas wanted gold, and got his wish. Everything he touched, even his daughter, turned to gold. Hitler wanted power, and in the end he had the power to bring his whole nation to disaster. Any desire may become King and rule all others. Alcohol or drugs may take over, and men become addicts and alcoholics. A simple thing like wanting a friend may torment you, so that you are in utter misery if someone doesn't notice or choose you.

We are strange creatures. Something, or someone, will finally get us. And the only safe course is to have God get us. He made us and He redeemed us—He owns us. If He can be King of our lives, all these other things, good in themselves, will fall into their proper place.

YEARS OF CHOICE

These college years are decisive ones. Many of you will choose vocations, but this is not the most important choice. If you will choose God, or let God choose you, the great decision will have been made. If you will become His disciple indeed, He most surely will open ways, in whatever vocation, for you to organize your lives around causes and purposes that are noble.

As a young member of the British Parliament, Lord Wilberforce's deep Christian loyalties made him pit himself against England's terrible traffic in slaves. After a lifetime of tireless struggle, he won the fight. The day came when Parliament met to pass the law forever outlawing the slave-trade. The younger Pitt took the floor and concluded his brilliant address with these words: "I am thinking tonight of two heads and two pillows. One is the head of Napoleon, tossing restlessly on his pillion at Helena, after having left a trail of blood from Jena to Waterloo. The other is the head of a man whose hair is grey after a life-time struggle for a cause. If I were to choose, I would not choose the head of Napoleon, but the head that will rest tonight, after our vote is taken, on the pillow of Wilberforce." Wilberforce had lived and worked those many years under the orders of his King, Jesus Christ.

THE KEY TO LIFE

You may not have as dramatic a role given you by your King. But in every university, in every schoolroom, in every home, in every shop or office—there are people to be helped, causes to champion, tasks to be undertaken—for the King. And if you can put all the good things of life—work, pleasure, money, success—all under His command, you will have found the key to life.

There are all sorts of voices which will clamor against having Christ take over as King of your lives. The world sets standards and fashions that threaten to call the shots. Our own deep self-centeredness will raise protests. We will measure our needs against the prevailing culture that surrounds us.

WHAT DO YOU NEED?

Have you really ever asked yourself what you actually do need? Our America is the place of fabulous wealth. If the entire world were reduced to a city of 1000 people, sixty would be Americans. These sixty would earn half of the city's income and own half of the city's property. The other 940 people would have to divide the other half. The average among you will have at least ten times as many clothes and perhaps twenty-five times as much money as the average boy or girl in India or Africa. Many of these have never tasted ice-cream; many will die early for want of simple food. We need to ask ourselves, "How much do we really need?"

Tolstoy tells the story of Pakhom, a Russian peasant. He lived on a small farm with his wife and sons. They were contented and happy. They had enough land. Then someone began taunting Pakhom for not having ambition. He ought to want more land, they said. Ambition began to eat away. He sold his farm, moved east, bought larger acres, worked night and day, added more land. The whole family worked from morning to night; they no longer had time for one another or for their neighbors. Finally, they moved still farther east to the foothills of the great mountains. There Pakhom drove a bargain with a wandering tribe of Bashkirs who owned all this country. For all the money he had, Pakhom could get all the land that he could walk or run around from sun-up to sun-down in one day. The next morning, at daybreak, he started out. In his eagerness for land, he set himself too large an enclosure. As the sun reached the horizon and was to set, he sighted the Bashkirs cheering him on to the finish. Exhausted, his feet like lead, pain making him almost blind, he pushed on. As the sun sank, Pakhom, twenty feet from the goal, stumbled and fell. The blood gushed from his nose and mouth. The Bashkirs shallowed out a grave, 6 feet long, 3 feet wide and 3 feet deep, and buried him. And Tolstoy adds, "And that's all the land that Pakhom really needed."

In all our talk about our need of clothes and cars and boats and even riding horses, we in America need to ask ourselves seriously, "How much does the King think we really need?" He has said, "To whom much is given, of him shall much be required." And so long as we have a single brother on this earth in want, we will have to give account for that which we have.

STEWARDSHIP IN MAKING FRIENDS

It is wonderful to have friends. You will make life-long friendships here at the University. They will be among the dearest in life. But even here, the stewardship of the making of friends will have to be under the rulership of the King.

You can pick your friends in two ways. You can find the kind whom you can use, who can do you favors. You can find the kind who need you, on the other hand, those who can use you, whom you can help. You need both kinds. But as a Christian who does things the way his King does things, you will certainly be on the look-out for people who need your help. There are people in every school who are lonely, discouraged, perhaps ill-tempered and therefore unpopular —people who need friends desperately. Your King will ask you to be on the look-out for them. Christ came not to be ministered unto but to minister. He didn't need you. He came to you because He knew you needed Him. You needed Him for forgiveness, for courage, for comfort, for hope. He died on a cross for you—so that He could help you. Then He went on to tell you that if you wanted to be His friend, to befriend Him, you should transfer your friendship to anyone who was in need.

NO NEED FOR SHAME

In one of the catacombs under the city streets of Rome there is a faint inscription on a damp stone wall: "Alexos loves Jesus." We don't know who Alexos was, perhaps some young man. Who etched this statement, we don't know, perhaps someone who wanted to taunt Alexos for his faith. The proud legions of Rome are now gone, the emperors lie in dust. But Alexos's friend, Jesus Christ, has gone on from one triumph to another, reshaping the civilizations of two thousand years. This great institution where you have the high privilege to study, is but another symbol in the triumphant march of this Christ and His Church down through the years. People may taunt you, too, for your friendship for your King. But He is King of all kings and will rule still when this earth is no more. No need to be ashamed of Him.

Also in the first century there was another young man, Saul. Brilliant, rich, the rising young star in the Jewish parliament, he was pegged as a leader for his people. Then one day, on a trail between Damascus and Jerusalem, Jesus came to him in a blinding light. He turned his back upon his career, became a persecuted, vagabond preacher, going up and down the countries of the Mediterranean basin telling people of this new Friend and King. The centuries have given their verdict. Nero was the emperor, and Paul the penniless apostle. But today people name their dogs Nero, and millions of mothers have proudly named their sons Paul.

WE NEED A KING

We, too, need a King—Paul's King. More than health or money or success—we need this King. Having Him may cost us our health and money and success. No matter! For with this King we have a Kingdom. We belong to a company of angels and archangels and all the hosts of heaven. We have on earth a power that nothing can match. "Crowns and thrones may perish, kingdoms rise and wane, but the cross of Jesus constant will remain." Death itself can do no more than end our assignment here on earth. When death had done its worst, our King will put us on our feet again in another part of His vast empire and give us new and wonderful work to do.

But as long as we are here on earth, He gives us work to do here. The earth is the Lord's. Everything is His. He is King of earth as well as of heaven. Your brain and your body are His. The governments, the labor unions, the factories, the schools, the newspapers and television net-works—all are His. Wherever you work, whether as a business man, a student, a doctor, a teacher, a farmer, a nurse, a factory hand, an editor, a congressman, a pastor—you work for the King. He is over every boss, and you do your jobs for Him because you are within His Kingdom.

And you don't wait until after graduation to take up assignments in His Kingdom. You don't rehearse for this role. The play is on. You are on the stage. The curtain may come down before graduation for you. The fulness of the Kingdom is yours right now, every hour. Enjoy the King to the full, work hard for Him, give every day all you've got. Then some day, soon or late, He will usher you into the glory of this everlasting Kingdom.

DR. GUILFORD L. HOLLINGSWORTH
Director, Boeing Scientific Research Laboratories

DR. HOLLINGSWORTH gave this lecture March 14, 1961, on a day's program devoted to the role of the sciences in contemporary life.

The Impact of Space Exploration

THE TITLE OF MY TALK TONIGHT IS "The Impact of Space Exploration." I think you will all agree with me that the advent of space exploration is one of the most exciting events within the memory of most of us. In many ways, it is analogous to the first successful flight of an airplane by the Wright brothers and if the analogy carries through we can be assured that the coming generation will be a generation of space enthusiasts. Now, if space exploration is going to make major changes in the lives of a whole generation of us, it is important and worthy of some detailed examination, and that is what we are going to try to do tonight.

Let's begin with a little bit of history in order to put the subject into proper focus. It is not quite clear when man first began to dream of exploring the heavens but there is some evidence that the dream did not exist as long ago as 600 years B.C. The Odyssey of Homer was written about that time and, although it is a most imaginative document, it makes no mention of travel into space. As long ago as 300 B.C., however, Aristarchus of Samos realized that our planetary system was centered around the sun, and he had some grasp of the size of the solar system and hence the possibility of its exploration. Once these fundamental ideas became clear in the minds of men it did not take long, as time is reckoned, for the dream of space exploration to crystallize. In 120 A.D., Lukius of Samos wrote the first book concerning a voyage into space. This book, *A Voyage to the Moon,* was in many ways a forerunner of "Gulliver's Travels," since it satirized important people of Lukius' time by caricaturing them in an imaginary environment on the moon. Lukius had a powerful imagination, indeed, since he found it necessary to include a brief disclaimer in the prologue to the book indicating that the voyage was entirely imaginary and he really hadn't been to the moon at all.

Space exploration was written about and discussed with various degrees of enthusiasm and accuracy for eighteen centuries after that, but most of us still felt that the work of even such recent investigators as Robert Goddard and Willy Ley were just as imaginative as that of Lukius until on October 4, 1957, a group of Russian scientists hurled into orbit the first artificial satellite of the earth, and gave it the imaginative name of "Sputnik."

The events that occurred on the following day are an illustration of what I am trying to convey by the use of the word "impact" in connection with space exploration. Certainly the impact on international politics was quick and dramatic. I believe the phrase in use at the time to describe its effect on certain of our government policies was known as "agonizing reappraisal." In the field of science, Sputnik was greeted with unrestrained enthusiasm. For the first time we had some actual measured data on the properties of the upper atmosphere and after Sputnik had made a few dozen circuits around the earth, precise observations of its orbit began to tell us some new things about the shape of the earth. In the field of economics, the impact was to be just as drastic, but its effect was hardly as noticeable. One by one new industries sprang up, calling themselves by one name or another, that indicated their connection with the suddenly respectable business of exploring space. And the "space age"—as it is popularly called today—had begun.

Four broad areas

I want to discuss with you tonight some examples of the impact of space exploration in four broad areas: the sciences, engineering and technology, economics and national affairs, and last and briefly, international affairs. Before I do this, I think it is necessary to define what I mean by space exploration. First, I am talking about exploration by means of vehicles of one sort or another, actual physical objects. While the sort of exploration that Lukius conducted is still going on, any prediction of either its course or its effect is far beyond my powers. Second, I want to limit the kinds of vehicles we are talking about to speeds not exceeding one-tenth the velocity of light and this rather automatically limits our exploration to the sun's planetary system and its immediate environs. Finally, I want to exclude such vehicles as intercontinental ballistic missiles from tonight's discussion, since both ends of their journey are right here on earth and their trip through space is purely incidental to their purpose.

Let us turn first to the area of the sciences in attempting to assess what space exploration has done or will do in changing our way of life. The most obvious areas of science to suffer change would be those of geophysics and astrophysics since they are concerned with such broad matters as the size and shape of the earth and the general mechanics of the universe. Some of the results in these areas are known to most of you, but it will be helpful to recite them here to put us all on a common footing.

SPACE IS NOT EMPTY

One of the first things to be found out about space is that it isn't! That is, space is not empty, but instead contains structures of unusual and beautiful shape and at least in the vicinity of earth, is swept by occasional fierce "winds" of solar particles. The structures I refer to are, of course, the well-known Van Allen belts that surround the earth approximately at its equator. The inner of these belts lies at a height of about 2,000 miles above the earth and is about a thousand miles thick in its most intense region. The outer belt is very much larger and is situated about 10,000 miles above the earth in the plane of the magnetic equator. It is about 4,000 miles thick and you might visualize a section through it as being crescent-shaped with the inside of the crescent facing towards the earth. It is not quite clear what sort of particles these belts consist of but the inner belt is almost certainly composed largely of protons; that is, the charged nuclei of hydrogen atoms. The outer zone seems to be quite different in makeup and probably consists largely of electrons. The origin of these particles has not yet been determined, although there is considerable evidence to support the view that the inner belt is the result of spontaneous decay of neutrons produced by cosmic rays. The outer belt probably results from trapping by the earth's magnetic field of the gas projected from the sun during violent solar storms.

As satisfying as it is to learn more about the nature of the universe in which we live, the real impact of space exploration on these sciences is that, for the first time, we are able to base our conjectures and theories on direct observation rather than on deduction alone. What is perhaps even more important, we are now on the threshold of an area where it is possible to make experiments in astrophysics. This is an event of the utmost importance in our continuing search for knowledge about the earth and the solar system. The importance of experiments in this difficult field of investigation can be best illustrated in the following way. All of us have, at one time or another, seen a beautiful display in the northern skies—the aurora borealis, or northern lights. The origin of these spectacular displays has been the subject of much speculation, and several theories have been advanced as to their cause. All of these theories have, of necessity, been based on indirect evidence, such as physical reasoning and observation of related effects such as magnetic storms and radio blackouts. One of the theories suggested that these effects were produced when a storm on the sun sent a burst of electrons speeding toward the earth in such a way that they were trapped in the earth's magnetic field and formed a temporary structure much like one of the Van Allen belts. Unlike the Van Allen belts' electrons, these electrons shuttle from North to South in their magnetic trap. Some of them escape at each end, and in colliding with the atmosphere, produced the glowing displays. Nicholas Christofilos of the Lawrence Radiation Laboratory at the University of California suggested in October of 1957 that this matter should be settled by means of an experiment. The experiment involved the creation of an artificial cloud of electrons at the right place in the earth's magnetic field by means of an atomic bomb. The possibilities of this experiment were so exciting that it was put into operation in a remarkably short time. On the 27th of August, 1958, an atomic bomb was exploded at an appropriate altitude a few hundred miles above the earth and the first man-made aurorae were observed. Actually, both northern and southern lights were produced since there was a brilliant auroral display over the south Atlantic in the vicinity of the Azores. Thus, as a direct result of our first efforts in space exploration, geoastrophysics and astrophysics entered a new phase, that of experimentation. For the first time in man's long history of his study of the heavens he has been able to confirm a theory concerning a major natural phenomenon, with a direct experiment.

From geophysics and astrophysics we turn now to astronomy, perhaps man's most ambitious quest, since through astronomy we hope to gain some grasp of the structure of the universe, its size and shape (if it has one) and some knowledge of its history since its beginning. The importance of space vehicles to astronomy and their impact on its progress occurs in two principal areas. Although most of us find it otherwise, the atmosphere, to an astronomer, is a murky and smothering blanket that has, since the beginning of time, prevented him from getting a good look at even the nearest of our heavenly neighbors. As you know, light, radio waves, x-rays, cosmic rays and all other sorts of radiation are forms of electromagnetic energy. In the last several decades, scientists have been able to devise instruments sensitive to electromagnetic radiation over a simply enormous range of frequencies. If we borrow a term from music, this range extends for some 60 octaves, extending as it does from the very longest radio waves at the extreme low frequency and to the incredibly short cosmic rays at the extreme high frequency end. Over this whole vast range of frequencies, our atmosphere is transparent only through a narrow band, some two octaves wide, that contains visible light, and a wider band, some 16 to 18 octaves wide, that represents its transparency to radio waves. All other frequencies, and some of these certainly contain the most interesting information about the universe around us, are either reflected or absorbed by our atmosphere. When we are first able to put a rather large telescope into a satellite, and with it take "pictures" of the sky around us, utilizing radiation at some of these forbidden wave lengths, especially in the ultraviolet, we shall be another step closer to a better understanding of the universe around us.

The other aspect of astronomy, or perhaps more properly astrophysics, on which space exploration will have its most powerful impact is that branch which deals with the abundance of the elements. Central to any general theory of the development of the universe is an explanation of how and in what relative quantities the 92 elements were formed from the fundamental particles such as electrons, protons and neutrons. Some of this information is, of course, available through spectroscopic studies of the sun and other stars. Man, however, being the self-centered creature that he is, is especially curious concerning the formation of our planetary system. Since none of the planets are hot enough to emit light, the spectroscope can be of no help to us here. Thus, one of the most exciting events in science will occur when some manned or unmanned satellite brings back from the moon or one of the planets the first actual samples of material such as rocks, dust, and atmospheric gases, for here again we can confront astrophysical theory with direct experimental evidence.

Even more exciting than a collection of Martian rocks will be a collection of Martian or Venusian life. While evidence is available in almost overwhelming amount to indicate that life in forms quite similar to those found here on earth cannot exist on other planets, the qualification "quite similar" is an unnecessary and crippling limitation. Just as man and all the other creatures of the earth have, over the thousands of centuries, adapted themselves to their own special environment, so probably have other forms of life adapted themselves to the environment on the planets where they exist. It would indeed be difficult to over-dramatize the impact on the life sciences of the return to earth of the first living material from one of our other planet neighbors.

METEOROLOGY

At this point in the discussion you may well feel that the entire aspect of space exploration is directed outward, away from the earth, and deals largely with things at a great distance. To a considerable degree this is true, but one of the most important impacts of space exploration will occur very much closer to home. For a long time, man has observed, studied, and attempted to describe the circulation of the atmosphere in an effort to improve his ability to predict the weather. This is an extremely difficult task, since our ability to observe the motion of the atmosphere is painfully small, limited as it is to a few hundred weather observation stations, balloons, and aircraft operating at widely separated points. Some idea of the complexity of this circulation pattern can be gained by a simple experiment and one that you can readily conduct at home. The only apparatus that you need is a cup of hot, black coffee, and a table on which to place it. You must seat yourself in such a position that the light from some source, preferably a window, is reflected on the surface of the coffee. By this means, you can see the motion of the patterns made by the tiny oil globules floating on the surface. These motions are caused by such processes as convection, diffusion and evaporation and thus are closely related to the processes that bring about the motion of the atmosphere. If you watch closely, you will see a miniature jet stream, a thin line of particles, start out across the cup, gather speed and perhaps wrap itself into a miniature cyclone, but I wager that, no matter how long you will look, you will find yourself unable to predict where the next one will take place or when, or whether it will terminate in a little cyclone or just wear itself out in a lazy, undulating motion. Systematic observation, by satellites such as Tiros, of the patterns of the clouds, as they move in the earth's atmosphere, will one day surely give us the key to a clear understanding of this important phenomenon. Now, you might feel that this impact is limited to another of the physical sciences, namely meteorology, but this isn't the case. Assume, for example, that the government is in a position to predict for many months in advance the major events of the weather. What sort of action will we take when it is clear there will be two successive years of drought over a major farm area with the resultant near economic disaster? What sort of action can, and should, the government take with respect to the people who live in that area? And, for that matter, will it be able to convince them in adequate time of the need to take something other than a "wait and see" attitude? Consider the situation when the government of, say, a small country finds itself in possession of information concerning a major natural disaster, but the resources to cope with it are simply not at hand. Will the officials seek to suppress the information, or will they blame the whole affair on some secret weather modification scheme of a rival country and thus lead their nation into war? Or, realizing that this same information is in the hands of other nations, find themselves compelled to seek a treaty of alliance in order to obtain the necessary resources to avoid widespread suffering? Certainly the impact of space exploration falls in the area of social sciences and highlights our need to know more about attitudes and how they are formed, about economics and geopolitics, and particularly about communication, so that we can convey our ideas and concepts and not merely words to the minds of people.

RESEARCH MUSHROOMING

Let us turn now from the area of the sciences to that of engineering and technology. A hurried perusal of many of the engineering journals published today might lead you to believe that all of our engineering and technology are simply by-products of space age research and that previous to October of '57, we were an agrarian nation with little or no engineering capability. Extreme as it may seem, this view is not without some foundations. A recent report of the Committee on Science and Astronautics for the United States House of Representatives points out that there are now at least five thousand companies and research organizations engaged in the missile and space industry and that these companies and their affiliates produce more than 3,200 different space-related products. In the same publication, one finds that the venerable National Advisory Committee on Aeronautics has been modernized into the National Aeronautics and Space Administration and now has some 18,000 employees studying the problems of man's exploration into space. Certainly all this activity will have some major impact on engineering technology, although it will surely fall short of my facetious introduction on the subject.

Strides in Communications

For rather obvious reasons, one of the areas in which space exploration will have its most immediate impact is that of communications. Certainly if we are able to communicate with satellites, and with deep-space probes cruising in the vicinity of Mars, we will have made some big strides forward in communication equipment itself and thus it is fairly safe to predict a substantial improvement in our ability to communicate between two points here on the earth. This change will come about from the improvement of the equipment itself, and of course, from the employment of satellites as relay stations. This scheme will allow us to escape the line-of-sight limitations ordinarily imposed on very short wave or microwave transmissions. The era of satellite communications has just begun on a commercial scale with the recent announcement that the American Telephone and Telegraph Company intends to request permission of the federal government to launch and operate satellites as part of a worldwide communications system. Initially, this sort of communication will be limited to relatively long distances, for example, about 3,000 miles and to over-water routes, where alternate means of communication are inadequate. To most of us, the transatlantic telephone service probably seems at least adequate, and for me it is a bit more than adequate since I haven't found a need for it yet. Actually, there are only about a hundred simultaneous transatlantic telephone channels available at this time and these are barely enough to serve the growing needs of our international relations and our international commerce. A large proportion of these 100 channels employ short-wave radio with the attendant dangers of interruption due to violent storms, both on earth and on the sun.

There has been a great deal of talk about the cultural and political importance of international television circuits and this matter is quickly brought into focus when one realizes one television channel requires the equivalent of a thousand telephone channels or about ten times the total transatlantic capacity now existing! Increasing this capacity by an almost indefinite amount is a relatively easy job for a satellite of the reflector types, since the only requirement placed on the satellite is that it be in view of both the sending and receiving stations throughout the duration of the transmission. To provide 24-hour continuity of service we of course need a number of satellites, so that the transmission can be switched from one to the next as they successively pass overhead. Although such satellites are simple and reliable, they impose severe requirements on ground equipment, as compared to the use of satellites that contain a receiver and transmitter. When equipment for these satellites becomes sufficiently reliable they will certainly be used but their use will pose an interesting problem in international relations.

It will be necessary to have some sort of an international federal communication commission to set technical standards for the equipment carried aboard since it is likely that it will be in use by several nations simultaneously if the satellites are to serve their purpose efficiently. Some interesting problems in regulations will arise since it will be possible for one nation to overtax the capacity of the satellite and thus deprive another of its vitally needed communications channels. These problems are mostly technical and there is already a growing record of successful solution of technical problems on an international basis. The solution of these more difficult ones, and the drafting of their attendant regulations will bring us one step closer to international cooperation.

If one traces the growth of business on an extended autonomous basis in the United States, there is a striking parallel with the growth of the transcontinental telephone system, together with its attendant teletypewriter and facsimile services. Indeed, some investigators believe this to be simple cause and effect and point out that the present autonomous operation of most large multistate businesses would be totally impossible without our modern, high-speed communications systems. Some organizations have gone so far as to carry all their accounting operations at a central location with the raw data being fed by wire into a computer at the instant it is recorded at the various outlying factories and stores. It is clearly within the capabilities of satellites to provide the same level of communication on an international basis that exists in the United States today. One is tempted to predict that a parallel growth of international businesses will take place, with the eventual result that giant companies having operating plants and divisions located all over the world will develop.

The staggering size of some of these predicted communications systems is illustrated by a prediction by Lloyd V. Berkner, a member of the President's Science Advisory Committee, when he said, "Within 10 to 15 years, the annual dollar volume of the satellite communications business will be on the order of one hundred billion dollars." In thinking about such a number, it might be well to recall that the current national budget stands at about 81 billion dollars and the gross national product at about 500 billion dollars. Even if Mr. Berkner is wrong, by as much as a factor of ten, the word "major" will be an inadequate way to describe the impact of space exploration on the communications business.

INTERNATIONAL TV

The prospects of international TV, rosy as they may be, merit a bit sharper look. The Londoner who wishes to

watch the 6 p.m. newscast originating live in New York will find himself up at the uncomfortable hour of 11 p.m., and this will probably dampen his enthusiasm for watching anything but the most earth-shaking events. One must consider also that the possession of a television set implies a certain standard of living and that the differences in the standards from those existing in the United States are even more drastic than the time differences. Finally, we must recall that the technical operation of TV can communicate only pictures and words, not ideas. Just as we find life in America poorly represented by the export of B-grade western films, so might we find it poorly represented by thoughtlessly produced television programs. Here again the impact of space exploration falls at least as heavily on the social sciences as it does on the physical sciences and engineering, for we will be ill able to use such technological revolutions as worldwide TV until we learn to communicate ideas and understanding as well as we communicate words.

Another area in which space exploration has had, and will continue to have, a substantial impact is that of structures and structural materials. While we are all aware of the need for exotic materials of all sorts to build space ships, it may be helpful to get a quantitative picture of the gap these materials must close. If we assume that an ordinary automobile weighs 3,000 pounds empty, when fully loaded with 800 pounds of passengers and a hundred pounds of fuel, it will weigh 3,900 pounds. If we divide the weight when full, 3,900 pounds, by the weight when empty, 3,000 pounds, we get a figure of 1.3, which in space-age language means that the automobile has a weight ratio of 1.3. This weight ratio is a fairly good measure of the difficulty of building a structure and of the quality of the materials required. Low weight ratio denotes easy-to-build structures, requiring simple materials, and high weight ratios denote difficult-to-build structures, requiring unusual, exotic, strong materials.

If we take another slightly less familiar example, the Boeing 707, we find that it weighs 125,000 pounds empty and 312,000 pounds when full, thus resulting in a weight ratio of 2.5. This is quite a bit more than that figure of 1.3 for an automobile and it is obvious that an airplane is quite a bit more difficult to build.

When we get to rockets, we find that even the venerable V-2 had a weight ratio of 3.2 and a fairly modern short-range ballistic missile has a weight ratio of 6.4, while if we wanted to get to the moon in a single-stage rocket, we need a weight ratio of 41.5. An automobile designed to V-2 weight ratio would weigh 410 pounds to carry the 900 pound payload. Some common structures have rather good weight ratios. If we weigh an ordinary can of beer when full, and then empty, and calculate the resulting weight ratio, it will come out about 5.4. In this instance, the beer represents the weight of the fuel for some imaginary rocket and the empty can represents the entire structure, the turbines that pump the fuel, the engines that drive the turbines, the propulsion engines, the communications system, controls, the gyros, and possibly the weight of the unhappy passenger. As we learn to design structures that meet requirements such as these, we will necessarily evolve some new and startling techniques useful wherever a strong, light structure is required. We will certainly develop some new, extremely strong materials, and learn a great deal more about the ways of intelligently using materials we already have.

ROCKET POWER PLANTS

One area that receives a great deal of attention these days is that of power sources for rockets, and it might be thought that the development of rocket power plants would have a major impact on areas of engineering technology related to motive power. To some extent, this is a case of mistaking the cause for effect, since any company that has a light, efficient power plant, whether it was originally designed for an outboard motor or part of the air conditioning system of a commercial airplane, finds it expedient sales-wise to indicate that this device was a direct outgrowth of some missile or satellite project. Rockets themselves are fundamentally very inefficient power plants unless they can be operated at speeds greatly in excess of those practical for flight within the atmosphere. For this reason, it does not seem likely that the continued development of more powerful rockets will have much of an impact on power plants for other forms of transportation.

Rockets, like other vehicles, however, have need for auxiliary power plants to produce electricity, pump fuel and compress air. If these power plants are to operate for months or even years in unmanned satellites, it is certain that they will make use of nuclear energy in one form or another, and thus it would appear that one of the principal impacts of space exploration on the power generation field may be the development of compact nuclear power plants. One would be ill-advised, however, to translate "compact" and "nuclear" into "inexpensive" since they may well be the most costly power plants produced for any purpose.

One final area of engineering that deserves brief comment is that of reliability. In this context, reliability is defined as "the ability to produce a device that will function in the prescribed manner in the environment in which it is used, for the prescribed length of time." In no other area of engineering are such strenuous efforts being made to produce extremely reliable components. Some of these components have a probability of failing within a design lifetime of less than one chance in a million. It is quite clear that, as the space exploration industry matures, one of its most important by-products will be vastly more reliable components for inclusion in a range of products reaching from automobiles to pocket transistor radios.

IMPACT ON OUR ECONOMY

I think it is now appropriate to turn our attention to the impact of space exploration on our economy, and to a certain degree, on our national affairs. While some measure of this impact may be understood from the previously mentioned figure of 5,000 companies engaged in the space age

74

business, that figure alone is subject to considerable inaccuracy. This inaccuracy comes about in a number of ways, not the least of which is that these firms are also engaged in production of many non-space age products. One measure of impact that can be put simply in figures is the amount of money that the government has spent or plans to spend on space exploration. Although the numbers themselves are sufficiently large so as to be difficult to grasp, they do afford a means of comparison with other forms of activity. Before we make specific dollar comparisons, it is important to realize that these comparisons should, but do not necessarily, include alternate ways of reaching the same objectives. First, there may be no other way in which a particular objective of the space program can be attained, or second, we may not be able to discover what the objectives of space exploration programs are.

Broadly speaking, we can group our space activities into three classes, according to whether the objective is (a) military weapons, (b) national prestige, or (c) scientific research. Of course, some projects may well be a combination of these but any comparison has its limitations. Some light on the objectives of our space program is shed by the National Aeronautics and Space Administration, the section concerned with policy and purpose states that "(a) the Congress hereby declares that it is the policy of the United States that activities in space should be devoted to peaceful purposes for the benefit of all mankind." This statement would seem to rule out military objectives, and leave us with a combination of national prestige and scientific research. However, further down in the same section, we find the words, "except that activities peculiar to or primarily associated with the development of weapons systems, military operations, or defense of the United States" and then the article goes on to assign these responsibilities to the Department of Defense. There is presently a bill under consideration that will modify the Act in such a way as to remove military weapons from the area of space exploration. For this and other reasons related to military security, we will confine our discussion tonight to the areas of national prestige and scientific research.

SPACE EXPLORATION BUDGET

First, let us take a look at the over-all budget for space exploration, and see what conclusions we can draw from that, without specifying our objectives. In a report to the 86th Congress by the Committee on Science and Astronautics, Representative Overton Brooks estimates that in the 1960's, the United States government will spend between thirty and fifty billion dollars on space exploration, and more specifically, the 1960-61 fiscal year budget for space exploration will amount to three and one-half billion dollars. Now, if that sounds like a lot of money it is only because it is. By way of comparison, we should note that this is approximately 4 per cent of the total national budget. The Bureau of Budget indicates that the Veterans' Administration, Department of Agriculture, and the group of activities comprising labor, welfare, commerce, and housing each receive about 6 per cent of the national budget, while those activities classed as natural resources receive only 3 per cent. It is also interesting to note that the figure of three and one-half billion dollars for 1960-61 is just about equal to the amount of money spent by all the institutions of higher learning for that same fiscal year. That is, in the fiscal year 1960-61, we are spending as much for space exploration as we are for education beyond high school. While these figures are, of course, quite general, I believe that they establish beyond doubt that the space exploration program has already had a major impact on our economy when viewed in terms of the federal budget.

Now let us for the moment assume that the principal purpose of space exploration is scientific research, or to put it another way, the accumulation of new knowledge. I think it is reasonable to assume that the pursuit of one kind of new knowledge is just as valuable as the pursuit of any other kind, so therefore it would be fair to compare our expenditure in space exploration with our expenditures that are directly related to other research and development.

RESEARCH AND DEVELOPMENT

The National Science Foundation, in a recent study of research and development in the United States, estimates that in 1960 we will spend about 12 billion dollars on all research and development activities of all sorts. That figure includes both government and private spending and includes space exploration. Thus we can see that the federal expenditures on space exploration amount to about one-third of the entire sum we spend on all other types of research and development each year in the United States. Many of you, I am sure, feel that space exploration is a sort of "blue sky" research, and therefore ought to be compared with basic, fundamental research rather than with all research and development activities. The Science Foundation report estimates that the expenditures on all basic research will amount to about one billion dollars. In making these comparisons, I want to emphasize again that the budget figures related to space research concern only money from the federal budget, whereas those figures describing the extent of our R&D activity in basic research represents funds from all sources, such as industry, government and educational institutions.

If we examine some of the details of the National Science Foundation report we find that their entire budget for the year is some 61 million dollars. Of this, some 25 million dollars is spent in support of research in medicine, and only 2 million dollars for support of research in the social sciences. While on the topic of medicine, it is interesting to note that space medicine expenditures will total about 23.5 million for 1961, as compared to 28 million for the American Cancer Society. I think it would be safe to say that if we feel the principal objective of our program in space exploration is one of accumulating scientific knowledge, then we are spending far too large a share on activities related to space exploration alone. In this regard, the director of the Lamont Geophysical Laboratory has remarked, "I think that we should be as interested in the ocean's bottom as the moon's backside." It is also unfortunately true that the glamour of space exploration projects attracts more and more people into careers in the physical sciences, and more and more money into support of activities in the physical sciences; at a time when the need for more top-notch original research in the social sciences is very great.

NATIONAL PRESTIGE

Another way of looking at the space exploration program would be to assume that its principal objective is to increase our national prestige. Indeed, the National Aeronautics and Space Act directs that the work of NASA should be carried on in such a way as to bring about "the preservation of the role of the United States as a leader in aeronautical and space science and technology, and the application thereof to the conduct of peaceful activities within and outside the atmosphere." Certainly, a recollection of the events following the successful launching of the Russian Sputnik and our own failures in the Vanguard program would do much to convince one that national prestige is certainly an important by-product of our space exploration program, if indeed it is not *the* objective. It is difficult to find in the national budget items clearly labeled "national prestige" against which we can make a comparison of the cost of the space program. One naturally thinks of the United States Information Agency, or Radio Free Europe, but the budgets of these organizations are so small as to make comparisons meaningless.

I am sure we hope for much more than prestige from our total expenditures on foreign aid, but even this budget, amounting to 3.4 billion dollars annually falls just short of the amount we plan to spend on space exploration. Although the public press lauds this situation and many of us feel that such expenditures are necessary in the interests of the national prestige, it is interesting to consider the following lines from the Annual Report of the Advisory Council on Scientific Policy, presented to the British Parliament by the Lord President of the Council. In the section relating to space research, we find the following words: "We have accordingly reconsidered the subject and reaffirm our previous advice, namely, that a program of scientific research in space using satellites on a purely national basis would not, in itself, justify the very large expenditures necessary for a full-scale program, including the development of a launching vehicle." This document, together with the apparent concurrence on the part of Her Majesty's government makes it clear that Britain does not feel that the space program can pay its way by contributing to national prestige or as a contribution to the affairs of science.

In considering this difficult matter of prestige, one has to bear in mind that what is a reasonable expenditure for one nation may be disastrous for another, and that it is not entirely fair to compare alternate ways of doing the job if the nation in question is sufficiently wealthy to use all of the ways simultaneously to insure reaching its planned objectives. It is also clear that a given course of action will not be viewed in the same light by all the nations of the world. It does not seem reasonable to expect that we should have the same influence on the underprivileged countries of the world with an elaborately successful program of space research as we might have on the well-developed industrialized countries. Certainly, if prestige is our objective, we must keep our intended audience in mind. Some countries are more impressed by a striking increase in the size of our ballistic missile program or the number of our Polaris submarines. This matter of national prestige is not only a subject for concern in our councils of state, but is a matter of responsibility and importance to each of us. This is a democracy and our nation is but the sum of the individuals who make it up. Thus we each bear responsibility for the face we turn to the rest of the world.

Effect on education

No discussion of our space exploration program would be complete without some mention of its effect upon the education and the schools. I am not aware of any other event that brought as much attention on the part of the average citizen to the problems of modern day education as did the success of the Russian Sputnik. Since that time, there has been a steady increase in interest on the part of parents and students alike in science, the schools, and school problems, nor has this interest shown any sign of waning. Public reaction to this event as to others that tend to disturb us, usually results in some overcompensation. This is the case in education also. For example, there has been a steady increase in enrollment of students in engineering and a slight decrease in the enrollment of students in the social sciences. Thus, although we are entering an era which will put increased demands on engineering, and on the social sciences, we are, at the same time, undergoing a reduction in the resources with which we can meet this demand.

Finally, I would like to make some observations concerning the impact of space exploration on some rather limited areas of international relations. One of the most encouraging aspects of this program has been the appearance of proposals for joint experiments involving the United States government and the British government; and more recently, joint experiments involving both the United States and Russian governments and their respective scientists. In general, these joint experiments have been successful and have shown that with a common objective, the people of all nations can work harmoniously together. In a recent news release, President Kennedy announced he has asked Llewellyn Thompson, our ambassador to Russia, to ask Premier

Khrushchev for a meeting at which the pooling of work on space exploration and medicine might be discussed, with a view towards increased areas of cooperation between the United States and U.S.S.R. Great events often proceed from small beginnings and the least that we can hope for from these joint efforts is a lessening of international tensions, and a growing better understanding between our two countries. Indeed, on a broader scale, it may be that space exploration will provide such a tremendous challenge to the energies of the major nations of the world that it will channel these energies towards a common goal, and thus greatly reduce the potential of war. Certainly, there is enough unexplored room in space to provide an adequate outlet for the "ruthless colonization" of which the United States and other free nations are often accused.

International laws for satellites?

The act of colonization dates back a great many years.
The symbolic planting of a flag on an unknown shore has often been taken in international circles as evidence of possession. The inclusion of a small Russian flag in the recent satellite launched towards the planet Venus leads one to wonder to what extent this principle can, and might, apply in space exploration. In a more serious vein, it is clear that the operation of satellites of various sorts will bring about new international problems, for which there are no adequate precedents. One of the most interesting of these is certain to arise shortly and will be similar in principle to the U-2 incident. In connection with that affair, it is important to recall that the U-2 type aircraft made a great many flights over Russia and these flights were observed by the Russians and it is reasonable to assume their purpose was known. No protests to these flights were made, apparently since the Russians were unable to intercept them and did not wish to make this fact public by protesting such unauthorized flights over their territory. At this very time, or in the near future, satellites of both Russia and the

United States will be circling the earth taking pictures of the territory below. Will these flights become a basis for international protests and diplomatic notes, or will each nation remain silent until they have developed the capability of destroying satellites of other nations?

Further, what will be the international status of such action, if taken against a satellite belonging, say, to the United States? What sort of hunting laws shall we propose for the bagging of supposedly spying satellites? May we shoot at them over international territory such as the high seas, or shall we be required to confine our shooting to our own back yard, as it were? The laws of men will here have to be tempered with the laws of physics, for satellites do not fall down when hit and perhaps a successful intercepting shot will have to be fired once around the world in the opposite direction to the offending satellite, such that a mid-space collision will occur over, say, our own territory. What then, is the legal status of the intercepting satellite as it passes over Russia on its intended lethal journey?

Perhaps these questions are not the important ones, but questions will have to be asked and answered concerning the status of the various kinds of satellites that will encircle the earth on photographic missions. In finding answers to these important questions, it is clear that we will have to discard old attitudes and search for new ones. Again, the impact of space exploration falls outside the physical sciences! Solutions will not be found in minor adjustments to previously existing arrangements or in legal hairsplitting that attempts to find a precise middle-of-the-road course of action. The recent administration proposed a plan that was essentially "open skies" inspection of communist territory by those of the free world and vice versa. There were a variety of reasons why this plan was not acceptable. Recently, a friend of mine proposed an imaginative solution to this problem involving the use of satellites, and it may well serve as an illustration of the kind of approach that may be necessary. His idea, in essence, involved the launching of several camera-equipped satellites by the United States.

These satellites would circle the globe at suitable latitudes, photographing the territory beneath them. The photographs would be retrieved by the United States and printed, together with suitable map coordinates. The photographs would then be made available to all those who wished them by the Coast and Geodetic Survey at a cost that would be essentially nominal. Thus any nation could, for a modest expenditure, acquire an excellent photographic atlas of all the defense and offensive installations of any other nation, and spying of the ordinary sort would be rendered unnecessary and overly expensive. Here again the impact of space exploration will occur in areas other than the physical sciences and the implications with respect to education and the public interest do not need repeating.

We have seen in this brief discussion how space exploration will have an impact on several areas in both expected and unexpected ways. At the risk of over-generalization, I would like to sum up its impact if I can, in a somewhat more compact way. A principal and by far the most important, impact of space exploration is that it represents the last step, if you will, in the fusion of science with government, and of government with science. If our democracy is to survive in the space age, we, as citizens must accept the responsibility of being literate in the affairs of science, and we, as scientists, must accept an equal responsibility of being literate in and taking part in the affairs of the government. The time remaining in which we must seek for and find a peaceful solution to the world's problems is perilously short. If the glamour of space exploration does nothing more than communicate to the average citizen a sense of urgency and responsibility towards this situation, it will have been worth all the cost.

BIBLIOGRAPHY

1. "The Impact of Space Activities on our General Economy" by Dr. Homer J. Stewart, Director, Office of Program Planning and Evaluation, National Aeronautics and Space Administration. Presented to the Corporation, Banking and Business Law Section, American Bar Association, August 25, 1959, Miami Beach, Florida.

2. "The Interaction Between the Earth Sciences and Planetary Studies" by Gordon J. F. MacDonald, Theoretical Division, Goddard Space Flight Center, NASA, as part of symposium on Impact of Space Research on the Sciences, New York City, December, 1960.

3. "Extra-Terrestrial Life" by Philip H. Abelson, Geophysical Laboratory Carnegie Institute of Washington, D.C., as part of same symposium as (2) above.

4. "Watch for These Space Age Changes" by Brig. Gen. H. D. Paxon (U.S.A., Ret.) et al., *Nation's Business,* January 1959, pp. 67-76.

5. "Annual Report of the Advisory Council on Scientific Policy, 1959-60" presented to Parliament by Lord President of the Council and Minister for Science by Command of Her Majesty, October, 1960. (Printed by Her Majesty's Stationery Office, London) .

6. "The Practical Values of Space Exploration" Report of the Committee on Science and Astronautics, U. S. House of Representatives, 86th Congress, Second Session, Pursuant to H. Res. 133 (Serial I) . (Printed by United States Government Printing Office, Washington, 1960.) July 5, 1960—Committed to the Committee of the House on the State of the Union and ordered to be printed.

7. *The Exploration of Space,* A symposium on Space Physics (April 29-30, 1959) sponsored by the National Academy of Sciences, The National Aeronautics and Space Administration, The American Physical Society. Edited by Robert Jastrow, The MacMillan Company, New York—1960.

8. "U.S. Aeronautics and Space Activities, January 1 to December 31, 1959." Report to Congress from The President of the United States, Dwight D. Eisenhower, February 22, 1960.

9. "Proposed Studies on the Implications of Peaceful Space Activities for Human Affairs" by Donald N. Michael. A Report prepared for the Committee on Long-Range Studies of the National Aeronautics and Space Administration by the Brookings Institution, Washington, D.C., December, 1960.

84

DR. S. C. EASTVOLD
President, Pacific Lutheran University

DR. EASTVOLD gave this lecture on Christian
College Sunday, April 16, 1961

Christian Education — Stand Up
and Be Counted

TEXT: *"Ye Shall Be Witnesses Unto Me"—Acts 1:8*

WE HAVE COME TOGETHER in one of the most ominous and
epochal hours in the life of the world. Stupendous influences and forces are shaking the world to its very foundations. When we were in Africa in 1958, we contemplated
the future, and what we expected to be happening twenty-
five years in the future has already come to pass in less
than three years. All these conditions pointedly remind
us how desperately we need great teachers to be the pre-
ceptors of the nations of the world.

Frightful chapters are being prepared for the pen of the
historians. There are intense violations of the age-old doctrine of the separation of Church and State. We might

wonder if the unyielding battle for liberty, fought by our forebears, is being lost today. We remember how they dared to be odd, to stand alone, to refuse to conform, though it cost them suffering and even life.

As we gather here as friends of Pacific Lutheran University, I take it that we want to encourage education which will inspire those who are seeking to achieve high goals. We must not be content to challenge and criticize the Soviet Union unless we make an effort to take a lead as Christian people. We dare not bury the great ideals of America and the Christian Church under our own timid spirits. The cries of revolt around the world must not fall on deaf ears. It will be impossible for us to sit back and enjoy our freedoms while more than half of the world is in spiritual and moral darkness.

PACIFIC LUTHERAN UNIVERSITY HAS A GOOD LOCATION

Pacific Lutheran University has a splendid location, in a great community, for a real conservative and aggressive program in Christian higher education. Only lethargy and shortsightedness can defeat us.

The greatest service of Pacific Lutheran University is in the future, and that future is in our hands today. We may likely write more history in the next ten years than we have in the past 70 years. God has placed an open door before all Christian institutions of higher learning today.

It would be impossible for me to speak of the many material needs which face us, as they do many other Christian colleges in America. As sure as God wants this school here, our needs will be supplied: materially, educationally and spiritually. It has always been the hope and prayer of the leaders and supporters of this school that the education given here will prepare young people for God's plan in their lives.

86

Colleges and young people are always interested in the future. The next ten years at Pacific Lutheran University are somewhat predictable—in a general way. The trends are ascertainable, not as to details, but in direction, and various basic factors are already firm. Population, for example; and various technological developments, for another example.

The next ten years have been referred to as *"The Soaring Sixties,"* or *"The Golden Sixties."* Economic advancement will be greater than at any time in our entire national history, even greater than the boom of the last decade, the boom that ran from '47 to '57. It appears that the boom should start in 1963-64 and run through the decade, accelerating at a fast pace in the final half, the last five years. Pauses in the progress, perhaps a pause in 1965-66, a mild recession, but the period as a whole will be essentially booming, the trend upward. Gross national income will be around 700 billion, showing a startling rise from its present level of about 475 billion. Employment, now 65 million, then 80 million . . . but at all times there still will be some unemployment—some industries out of kilter. This means that a lot of social problems will still be with us. People will have 50% more money to spend—actual buying power. The total business profits will probably be 45% above the present level. The price level ten years from now will probably be 15% or so higher than now. This is not too bad an inflationary prospect.

NO BIG WAR

Because neither side dares to start it, it is not likely that we will have a big war, unless the good Lord decides it is time to come back again. The number of houses built will rise from 1,300,000 a year to 2,000,000 a year. Total population will rise from 177,000,000 to 208,000,000. There will be a 40% increase in the 20 to 30-year-olds by 1970 . . . only ten years off. School agers, 6 to 19, will zoom, a rise of 25% in the next decade. There will be an increase in households from 51,000,000 to 61,000,000—a record-breaking rise. Marriages will rise from one and a half million a year to two and a half million a year, and in the seventies three million a year. There will be a great increase in vacation resorts, travel and sports. The leisure business will have a fantastic growth. People will live longer, and those over 65 years will increase by 30% in 1970. The public schools will be hit by the bulge of teen-agers. This means higher local taxes.

COLLEGES AND UNIVERSITIES

There will be twice as many students applying for entry to the colleges ten years from now. We need to expand as much in the next ten years in our colleges as we have expanded during the last three hundred years. We will not be able to do it that fast. There will likely be more public money, even for private colleges. Tuition will be higher. Someone has said, "With the rise in tuition, it is almost as expensive to be educated as it is to be ignorant." The government is already in the business of loaning money to students. Standards will be higher and screening will be tighter.

PRIMARY LEADERSHIP PROSPECTS

Our colleges will need to prepare more people in such professions as the following: mathematics, physicists, chemists, economists, accountants, engineers, physicians, draftsmen, teachers, lawyers, pastors and missionaries. There will be need for more sales people, more clerical and office workers, more skilled tradesmen to make more and more things that will be required by the public. We cannot, today, even imagine what will happen with the greater use of atomic and solar power. The air-conditioned automobiles will have permanent lubrication, and tires that will last the life of the car. There will be new miracle drugs and remedies for many common ailments. New super highways will change the face and flow of the nation. In fact, the whole world is speeding up in its development.

And who will bring this about? It will be the people who have trained minds, people with brains that are developed. Because of all of these changes, no one can plan his life and work in detail for the next ten years. But we can and must be aware of the trends that are already upon us.

A SHRINKING WORLD

Never before has a generation of University students been faced with the fact that this world has become very small. Today we have learned how to harness the atom. Tomorrow we are likely to find out how to influence the weather. Man has cultivated the land for millennia. We may soon find out how to cultivate the ocean. All of this will come about only in proportion as we cooperate with the rest of the world. There is going on today in the world a revolution of the *underdog of yesterday*. It is the revolution which has been called the revolution of rising expectations. It proceeds along the turbulent expansion of the industrial revolution over the whole world.

The education of the scientist is an integral and important part of the fateful decisions coming up. It would be a terrible thing if all of this development should get into the hands of de-Christianized or pagan minds.

Righteousness exalts a nation by the promoting of higher life of the spirit. There is a danger that wealth may persistently drag us down in a sort of gravity. When Rome was poor, she ruled the world; but when Rome became rich, she grew corrupt and fell. We must assert the fundamental and eternal worth of man, independently of his circumstances, with his feet on the ground, his head above the stars and his eyes upon God. We must teach man to do earthly things in a celestial way. To be great, we must have wealth, farms, factories, railroads, ships, air forces, but more than that, we must have solidarity. Most of all, we must have character in our people. This will be like the strong strands of steel that make the cable powerful. We must aim for the higher virtues of truth, honesty, sympathy, service, faith and faithfulness, which will reach down through the whole national life.

INSTITUTIONAL OBJECTIVES

Pacific Lutheran University has set up some real institutional objectives that are basically and soundly Christian. The object of the founders of this institution of learning was to provide a place where the young people can acquire a thorough education under Christian influences. This University will have no sympathy with that type of education which limits its objectives to this life only. We believe in teaching for the future, both in time and eternity. In all of this, the Bible, the Word of God, is to have a prominent place in all of our work and teaching.

The church college of today finds itself in the midst of two great conflicts. Being Church-owned, it is involved in the present great conflict which is being waged with respect to orthodoxy. Being an educational institution, on the other hand, it is also involved in the significant movement to enrich and modernize the curriculum of the liberal arts college. This institution is a *University,* and therefore ready to take its stand in the educational field and make a definite and valuable contribution. This institution is a *Christian University* and therefore gives a prominent place to the religion of Christ, with specific stress upon the need of living a life of service. This institution is a *conservative* Christian University, therefore it admits freely that it is giving preeminence to the great fundamental truths that humanity needs a Savior, that God is a personal, loving Father, that the Bible, as a revelation from God, is a more secure guide than the discoveries of science.

THE QUALITY TEST

The test of a college or university is the quality and not the quantity of its graduates. The Christian University cannot compete with our state-controlled universities in the number of its students. But it has every right in the world to be exceedingly proud of its men and women who today are assisting in building America. If religion is excluded from education, we will have no foundation on which to build moral character. Someone has well said: "Secular education deals with the head: Christian education includes the heart. Secular education gives men technical skill: Christian education adds social concern. Secular education points to the factories and skyscrapers: Christian education points to Christ."

THE WORLD IS IN A MESS

But is this all the world needs, more education and less ignorance? Even according to our most educated authorities, the world is still in a mess, in spite of our efforts to educate the populace. Merely sending our young people by the hundreds of thousands to universities and graduate schools is not going to solve the world's difficulties. Education alone is not the answer. Education must have a purpose behind it if it is to accomplish anything, and that purpose must be *Christian*.

A TROUBLED WORLD—PEACE

Our troubled world is seeking for peace, but does not find it. Peace is of the spirit and is not found in the material things of earth. Peace can come only in the hearts and minds of men. Such peace must come from God and can be delivered through the medium of Christian teachers.

The teacher cannot teach what he does not know. The teacher dare not pretend to the Christian point of life and yet remain uncertain as to its aims and purposes. We must not allow our Christian colleges and universities to be so ridiculously elective that any student can rush through without meeting Jesus Christ in our Chapel services as well as in the areas of the more academic courses. If such were ignored, then the "side-show will run away with the circus."

ARMED FOR GLOBAL WAR

The world is armed to the teeth for global war. The real enemy is spiritual. We face the question of survival. It may be the hour for God to take over and rule the world. We might well pray that God would hasten that day. That day is coming, or our religion is false. Even America will some day cease to be. We look for the coming of the eternal Kingdom. We must seek to prepare our students for that event. Humanity may destroy itself, and all that man has made, but the Word of God will endure forever and cannot be changed.

The survival of God is not at stake. The human race may become extinct, but God will not. God will survive all of man's blunders. Only those who are on God's side are safe. The road to survival is the road of faith and obedience to him. We must teach and live this doctrine and way of life. Our philosophy of education must never descend to the level of materialism. We must always be in the frontline of attack upon atheistic materialism. We are in the production line of Christian leadership.

A BULWARK

The Christian University must be a rampart, a fortification, a defender, a protector as over against all dangers to our precious heritage. There is a deadly and Satanic shift from the theocentric to an anthropocentric philosophy. It seems that man, not God, now occupies the greater part of man's plans. The result is an emancipation of divine contracts and conventional morals.

Even the State has a right to expect that we will send out

Christian citizens. We should be producing the "salt of the earth." If we fail, let it be only after we have given our lives in a serious effort to produce what God wants. It will require great devotion to face and accept this call.

FANTASTIC INCREASES

As we think of the unique function of the Christian university in America, we must be aware of the fantastic increases in the number of young people enrolling in our colleges and universities. In 1900, there were 214,000 students in American colleges. Estimates of future enrollments vary. According to the President's Committee on Education Beyond High School, there will be 6,000,000 college students by 1970.

The needs of an industrial, technical, scientific economy and culture have created an insatiable demand for knowledge and skill. Public institutions are preparing for great increases.

PUBLIC VS. PRIVATE EDUCATION

As Christians, we must have a renewed consciousness of our responsibility toward learning and learners. We are loyal members of the State, we are American citizens, and we take no second place to anyone in that category. However, where will we be with our ideals in education if education becomes increasingly under the control of the State? Even our state school leaders do not want that. As education is regarded more and more as an instrument of national policy, we wonder what will happen to education when it becomes more and more publicly controlled.

EDUCATE THE WHOLE MAN

We are living in a tremendous age. The challenge is so great that we might almost faint at the thought of it. It will be our duty, as supporters of Christian higher education, to strive to impart and to fulfill a particular philosophy of education.

93

Our first concern is to carry on colleges and universities of liberal education, and that means the education of the whole man and the whole woman. This cannot be done by dealing only with the body and the mind. It must by necessity include the soul. Because we have been faithful in these objectives, we have achieved for ourselves recognition as a clearly superior institution in the area of liberal arts and sciences in America.

MANY COMPETITORS

There are so many different kinds of institutions of higher learning today, that it is difficult to make any kind of comparison. It is regrettable that many of the institutions of higher learning among us today once held to the same great objectives which we still hold, but they have almost withered away into death. Some of them are spiritually dead. The great task of the Christian University, at which point I feel our University stands among those at the top, is to mediate Christian knowledge and to surround it with an atmosphere that will make it useful in the building of both the mind and the soul. It should be the task of Pacific Lutheran University to push back the horizons of the mind and the spirit of every student who will enroll here, and let those horizons include the eternal mansions of God.

As this University was born of the church, and possesses a great heritage that the State school does not have, and can never give, it has a unique place in our American life which no other kind of school can replace. We must always have the goal of competence, and the goal of faith which reveals eternity. Neither one of these goals is easy to achieve. Let us not lightly cast aside what has been accepted and tried for a long time.

I cannot over-emphasize the importance of acreage, buildings, laboratories, equipment, material evidence of strength, endowments and operating budgets, nor of the adequacy of beauty and comfort in dining halls and residence halls; but we must have something more than that to fulfill our unique position among the colleges in America today. Let us pray that we may continue to have great devotion to truth, untrammelled scholarship, integrity in the learning process, and to emphasize the spirit of honor, while giving no apology for intelligent religious faith. Our learning process is set up for some other reason than to further our own selfish aims, or even the aims of our nation or the welfare of mankind. We seek for divine approval and we do our work for the honor and glory of God.

A DARK WORLD

I wish to take the moments that are left to talk to you about the real business of Christian higher education, which means a witnessing as Christian educators before a materialistic world.

During the blackout in London in World War II, a reporter wrote that it was so dark that even the cats ran into each other. It is a dark world, but we witness to the fact that the Holy Spirit of God is at work in the world, and that the world is in his hands, and that God, who in the beginning created the Heavens and the Earth, is still creating. This faith lifts up our hearts and empowers our hands and minds to become co-laborers with him.

OUR GOAL—A NEW WORLD

A minister once astonished a meeting of his official board by ignoring the whole question of a balanced budget. He asked his leading church members: "Have you met God today?" There is a great University which has a sign across the door, "Little rooms where new worlds are made." I am thinking of the private chamber of the Christian professor who goes into the spiritual laboratory of his life, where new truths and new strengths are discovered and put to use.

In a small room in Independence Hall in Philadelphia in 1776, a new world was made when the Declaration of Independence was formulated and passed. A new world was made in a small room in Wittenberg, Germany, which was the study of Martin Luther. I am hoping that around in the offices and classrooms of Pacific Lutheran University are to be found places where Christian leadership is created.

ARE WE SMALL STUFF?

The Christian community of the Apostolic Age was a very small affair, and yet as we look back upon it, it was the biggest business of the generation. The Church of that century was so small that it could usually meet in the house of one of the members, and they were small houses. It might have been said that it was *"pretty small stuff,"* but history does not say that, and history will not say that Christian higher education in this generation was *"small stuff."*

The Secret Police in Jerusalem, reporting on the company of Jesus' disciples might have reported: "Don't worry. This movement will soon be over, there are only a few of them." There were only a few, but it was not soon over. The important thing was not the quantity, but the quality. The Coliseum held 100,000; the catacomb held only about 30, yet one has truly said that the catacomb was the "largest" place, for the little company meeting down there in the dark had the future on their side, because God was on their side.

Most of the Christian colleges and universities in America have been small. We have been small, and will continue to be in the minority. However, do not be deluded by the word "minority." That, so far as we can observe, has been the way God has always worked. The man, faithfully teaching as a Christian in the classroom of a Christian University, is a "big business man." The woman, bringing her love and skill into the work of teaching in the Christian sense, is a "big business woman."

Here, then, are some of the secrets of a growing, glowing Christian University, yesterday, today and forever. Herein will lie the secret of the future success of our Christian universities and colleges. We must tackle our job as parents, students, administrators and teachers in Christian higher education, with the consciousness that we need the power of God. Some colleges and universities that carry the Christian name never tackle anything more inspiring than balancing the budget, and many of them never even do that.

LET US MAKE BIG PLANS

When the Cathedral of Seville was being planned, the architect said: "Let us build a Cathedral so great that future centuries will think us mad for ever dreaming of it."

I am sure that there are people in this audience who are timorous and afraid. Let us together build an academic and spiritual University to the glory of God. Remember, Peter denied his Lord, because he followed "afar off." Unless we try to do things that seem "mad" to many onlookers, we are not true successors of the first century Christian educators, such as Paul and others. The Spirit of God empowered Martin Luther to defy the Holy Roman Empire and say: "Here I stand, I can do nothing else." The Spirit of God empowered John Wesley to face violent mobs with unflinching courage. The Spirit of God empowered fighters against the slave traffic in human slavery, even though they faced mob action and even death.

We are not responsible for success, but only for faithfulness in our witness to the truth. The most important question is not, "What is the world coming to?" but rather, "What has come to the world?" Let us not have an alluring substitute sort of "bootstrap religion," which puts psychology in place of religion. There is a flood of this in a hundred books on self-help, chasing our worries away, thinking pink and purple thoughts to overcome black thoughts, to pull ourselves out of all troubles by our own bootstraps.

CALL THE WITNESS—STAND UP AND BE COUNTED

"Call the Witness." These words mark tense moments in a trial in court. The early Christians were virtually told to

"take the witness stand." The verdict depended upon the testimony of the witness. They were called to "STAND UP AND BE COUNTED." That is exactly what the eleven disciples did at Pentecost. That is what the martyrs did in the Coliseum in Rome. This is what Christian professors must do if they are to have persuasive power. Let us be careful lest we develop the skillful technique of turning ourselves into "innocent bystanders."

Too many people in Christian institutions of higher learning are not so much fishers of men as they are members of a secret society sworn never to reveal aloud their faith in Christ for the work of their calling. At Pacific Lutheran University, we need to understand the meaning of this, "I will make you fishers of men." So far as Jesus Christ is concerned, he was the greatest Teacher that ever lived. He calls us to be teachers. He is not so much interested in having us teach the arts and sciences in the world which he created as he is to have us win men for salvation.

It is strange that such a clear, commanding invitation should be obscured; but it has been, time and again. We need to revive the priority of the "fishing business," the evangelistic purpose of the Christian University—when that great "first" becomes a second or third, even to such good things as a statement of belief, or the support of a visible organization, a benumbing sterility strikes the reason for our existence.

FINALLY

Christian education is important because education is life. It is a process which begins at the cradle and ends at the grave.

The ultimate aim of Christian education is to fashion men and women who can and will carry forward the insights made, and the achievements won, and who will go into the future with the firm conviction that they are claiming for Christ the Kingdom which is his. This includes standing for true science and research and discovery, as well as for the wide horizons of brotherly love and citizenship. There can be no tolerance of mediocrity.

To these noble ends and high purposes, I persuade you to "STAND UP AND BE COUNTED." Do this with your moral support, your financial support, and your prayerful support. We welcome you into this great crusade and fellowship. Amen.

DR. CARL F. REUSS
Director, Board for Christian Social Action,
The American Lutheran Church

DR. REUSS gave this lecture at the fourth annual
Family Life Conference, April 17 to 19, 1961

The Family in Perspective

OUR CONFERENCE THEME, "The Family—Apart But Not
Alone," reminds us that no family stands alone. Even though
an individual family be small, living in its own home, far
from relatives, and having little influence in its community,
nevertheless that family does not stand alone. Each family
is influenced by social behavior and community expectations, and in turn each family influences the standards, customs, and actions of its community. It is important to remember that no family stands alone.

Confronted by the patterns of behavior and expectations
in its community each family has three choices. It can actively support and re-enforce these patterns; it can actively
resist and seek to change them; or it can passively conform
to expected social behavior. In no case, however, can the
family ignore community expectations. The family simply
does not stand alone, nor can it stand alone.

Family life and behavior have been the subject of increasing study in recent decades. In reviewing the approaches and emphases of these studies we note various significant ways of looking at the family as a key unit in society.

FOUR APPROACHES

One approach sees the family as a unity of interacting personalities. The emphasis is upon the unity created by the action, reaction and interaction which takes place between and among the various members of the family.

A second approach sees the family as the place where husbands and wives, parents and children, and brothers and sisters live and function. Here the emphasis is upon the structure of the family, the functions it serves for family members, and the forms that family life may take.

A third approach views the family as the training and proving ground for life. The stress is upon persons, development of personality, and the effect that the ensuing stages of the family life cycle have upon the development of the several members.

A fourth approach emphasizes the family as a social institution, stressing the services and protections it gives its members in meeting basic human needs. Structure and function of the family are seen as satisfying not merely personal needs but also the purposes and needs of the community.

EMPHASIS ON GROUP PURPOSES

The fourth approach is the one I wish to emphasize in this particular address. Each approach has validity and justification. This year, however, by way of contrast to our usual American exaggeration of individual values, we wish to minimize the individual in favor of emphasizing group or collective purposes.

Every society needs institutions or systematic arrangements for organizing and regulating behavior which is intended to satisfy basic needs of both individual and society.

Regulating sex, reproduction, and child-rearing, providing for the interchange of labor and its products, insuring peace and order in the community, and relating man to the divine are examples of basic needs which have been institutionalized in marriage and the family, the economic order, government, and religion. We see them all as divinely ordained.

Thinking specifically of marriage and the family I would point out that in every society the family institution somehow must define, among other considerations, these fundamental rules:

Who may marry whom;
How the courtship process, if there is one, is conducted;
Who decides whether a specific marriage is permissible;
How the marriage ceremony is performed;
Where the newly married pair will live;
What the rights and duties of each spouse are;
How the children are to be reared;
Whether a marriage may be dissolved—and if so, how.

Precisely how each society defines these basic rules depends upon its own values and upon its own understanding both of human needs and of legitimate human aspirations. Each society believes that loyalty of its members to its definitions of right and wrong is essential to the very survival of that society. The behavior of each person is expected to conform to group standards and expectations—which of course for the individual eases decision making, gives group sanction to his action, and assures him favorable standing in the community.

If we understand this point we find it easier to understand marriage and family practices, even those far different from our own. Each set of these patterns has been adapted to the setting of a specific society, fitted into the total constellation of cultural practices, and been re-enforced by tradition and group sanction. Our own ways, for example, may seem not only alien but even beyond comprehension to a person reared in an entirely different cultural climate.

In this spirit of seeking to understand the family in perspective of different societies and cultures we can look objectively at various ways in which different peoples have defined the rules of social behavior governing the eight areas enumerated earlier. We see them as needed regulations of personal behavior which has both personal and social consequences.

Who may marry whom typically is defined by drawing lines or circles within which one may not marry and another set within which one must marry. Within the smaller circle one may not marry because the relationship is too close. Outside the larger circle marriage is forbidden because the persons are too different. One's marriage partner is drawn from within the larger circle. These principles deal with marriage of relatives by blood or marriage, persons of different races or religions, and even with the question of whether a person may have more than one spouse, as the practice of polygamy represents. Obviously various societies answer these questions quite differently, one from another.

How courtship is conducted also varies greatly from one society to another. Whether young people in courtship are free and unfettered, or whether under chaperones, whether restraints are imposed only after puberty, and even whether there is a courtship process are issues which various societies answer differently—but consistent with their whole outlook on life. The marriage even may be an arranged one over which the parties have no control.

Who decides whether a particular marriage is permissible may be the young people themselves, the parents of the boy, or of the girl, the larger family or tribal council, or perhaps the religious leaders. There is no universal human answer—but there is some kind of an answer given by every human community to this question of who gives approval to a particular marriage.

How the marriage is performed reflects especially the attitude which defines whether marriage is a religious or a civil affair, and whether it should be a quiet and simple ceremony or an occasion for feasting and celebration. Differences here are so well known as not to require further comment. The prime point is that our attitudes and values which define what marriage is become decisive in shaping the customs and traditions associated with the marriage ceremony itself.

Answers to *where the couple will live* may require them to join the man's or the woman's family, or separate them from both families and set themselves up independently in their own new living arrangement. Again, there is no universal answer, but universally some answer is given.

The defined rights and duties of husband and wife reflect whether the society is matriarchal, patriarchal, or perhaps equalitarian between the sexes. Everywhere, though, there are definitions of what men and husbands are to do, what women and wives are to do, just because they are men or women and wish to avoid losing their masculinity or femininity. The male and female roles in reproduction as yet are inescapable and non-transferable, but beyond this there are virtually no universal agreements as to what is essentially masculine, what feminine, in the division of rights and duties between the sexes in human life.

How are children to be reared? Are they taught respect for elders or do they expect to rule over households and adults? Are boys and girls reared separately or together? Are they reared by parents, by relatives, or by specialists assigned this function? The very raising of these and similar questions illustrates possible courses a given society may follow.

May a marriage be dissolved? Whether divorce is permitted, and by what process, each society answers in some fashion. In the event of the death of her husband what happens to the widow? Does she rejoin her parental family, join his family, continue in her marital home, or must she perhaps take her own life and accompany her husband into death? May she remarry, and if she does is her choice unrestricted or is it restricted—perhaps *to* members of her husband's family, perhaps *excluding* her husband's male relatives?

It would have been easy to mention what to us are lurid and sensational ways in which various societies have defined rules for regulating marriage and family life. These ways might easily have seemed to be bizarre, sexually lax, or sexually provocative customs. That would, however, have constituted a mocking or making sport of others, which is beneath us as Christians. Our emphasis deliberately was not on the bizarre or sensational. We want to look upon ways of answering these questions so differently from the way our society answers them as ways which are thoroughly responsible, socially consistent, protective of community interests, and at the same time personally satisfying. They simply are the customs specific societies have developed for meeting the persistent and recurring needs for regulating sex expression, reproduction, and child rearing.

FAMILY NOT UNIQUELY CHRISTIAN

Sometimes we need to be reminded, in connection with our interest in Christian family life, that the family is not a uniquely *Christian* institution. The family long preceded Christ's earthly ministry and the founding of the Christian church. Societies which never heard of Jesus Christ nevertheless have family life. The family, we declare, is part of God's order of creation, designed for man's good and the preservation and enrichment of human life.

What sets the Christian family apart is not certain forms or practices. Even Christians on different continents and in different churches do not necessarily agree on the specific forms or practices for regulating sex, reproduction, and child bearing. Much of what we claim to be inherently Christian in family life we may find on honest review is not much more than the effects of our cultural conditioning. We each may be partly right, and also partly wrong, as we interpret God's revelation of how He desires marriage and family relations to be lived.

What distinguishes the Christian family, it seems to me, are the sense of purpose and the spirit which prevail within the family and within the action, reaction, and interaction that take place among its members. At this point I should like to share with you thoughts formulated for the recent Lambeth Conference. The report of the special Committee on family life pointed out, not precisely in these words but in their spirit, that the Christian family is one where:

1. All yield themselves in disciplined and thoughtful obedience to the God who loved and redeemed them;

2. All bear common pain and share common grief, all give and receive equally of love;

3. All practice freely the choices life requires of them, within the protection of loving concern and watchful care;

4. Essential standards of judgment and discrimination are taught and followed;

5. All have learned to be themselves and to accept the individuality of others.

This phrasing obviously emphasizes the values and goals which dominate the Christian family. It is little concerned with forms and structures, but much concerned with the spirit and purpose which sets the Christian family apart from neighboring non-Christian families. Were we to take the time, many of us could think of other qualities we would want to add, especially of forgiveness, both sought and freely given.

In this period and in other presentations in this Family Life Institute we as a church people are demonstrating our intense interest in preserving, strengthening, and extending that divinely ordained institution we know as marriage and family. We see the family and its members not only as units and as personalities. We see the family also in the perspective of a social institution regulating human behavior in order to carry out and to fulfill basic individual and social needs in a manner consistent with the goals and definitions we believe God has established. He created man as a sexual being who needs companionship and who needs also the protections and security which orderly institutional arrangements give both to him and to his community. God wants to draw man back to Him through the adoption He offers in Jesus Christ. Our hope and our effort are that more families will live not only in the natural family relationship but also in the spiritually creative and nurturing Christian family.

DR. WILLIAM E. HULME
Professor of Pastoral Care, Wartburg Theological Seminary

Dr. Hulme gave this lecture at the fourth annual Family Life Conference held April 17 to 19, 1961

Family Life Crises and Sanctification

Our subject for this morning is *Family Life Crises and Sanctification.* I am sure you have a good idea of what a family life crisis is. Very few families are spared them. A gentleman about whose will I read in the newspaper while in England evidently had had quite a few of them. In his will he bequeathed his entire estate to his wife, with one stipulation: that she was to marry within one year of his death. The reason was he wanted to be sure that some-one else found out how hard she was to live with. Evidently his family troubles had little sanctifying effect. Now that we have family crises identified, what precisely is sanctification? Sanctification is a theological word which simply means our growing as Christians—our growing in faith, our growing in Christlikeness, our being sanctified, purified.

The Bible makes it very easy for us to relate sanctification and family crises because the Bible consistently expresses divine truths in comparison with family relationships both for purposes of analogy and of application. First as analogy. In order to get across to us divine truths like the nature of God and the kind of relationship that God establishes with us, the Bible uses family relationships as analogies so that we can get the point. Because we have had experience with human relationships such as family relationships, we get an idea from this experience of the heavenly relationships which are compared to them. There is also the purpose of application. Because we have the picture of God and God's relationship with us, we are able to judge the human relationship which has been compared to the divine. We know now what the human relationship should be like since our understanding of its divine counterpart offers the pattern. We know what God is like because we know what family relationships are like, and we know what family relationships should be like because we know what God is like.

Take marriage for example. It is used to describe the relationship between Christ and the church in the New Testament and the relationship between God and Israel in the Old Testament. Breaking faith with God was compared to infidelity in marriage. We can learn much about God's relationship with us because we know what the marriage relationship is. We can see the closeness and the intimacy and the confidence and the loyalty that exists between God and His people. Thus we learn much about Christ and His church because we know something about marriage. On the other hand, we know much about what marriage should be like because it is comparable to Christ's relationship with the church. We understand that a husband's love for his wife should be comparable to Christ's love for His church, in which He gave Himself up for it. And we know what a wife's response to her husband should be like because it is compared to the church's response to Christ.

Then there is the parent-child relationship where God is pictured as our Father and we are pictured as His children —a family situation. We are adopted, the Scripture says, into the family of God. God is the parent; we are the children. Again the point is that we understand what God is like to us because we know what human parenthood is like. We understand the divine relationship because we understand the human relationship between parent and child. Everybody has been a child of a parent. On the other hand, we learn a great deal of what parenthood should be like from the analogy of God as the divine parent. As an example: As we contemplate the character of God as Parent we see the parental wisdom that should be our pattern. Look at the wisdom of God as parent! God is very desirous to give, far more desirous to give than we are able to receive. At the same time in wisdom he awaits our asking. This is the whole basis of petition in prayer. God knows what we need before we ask, but He wants us to ask because it involves our participation. Also God is able to do all things. He can accomplish miracles but He depends on our doing, so far as the establishment of His purposes in this world are concerned. He uses us as the church and as society. Again He involves us. He develops us by putting us into action.

We have also a pattern of parental love as we see it in God's parental love. God is able to remove suffering from His children. He is able to take the cross from His children, but He does not always do it. Why? Because He wants to use that suffering, use that cross, to stimulate greater growth. God's love is always pushing us in the direction of our growth. God's love is unconditional in that it does not depend on any conditions that we must meet. God's very nature is love, and therefore His love depends only on Himself. We receive God's love on the basis of God and not on the basis of our qualifications. At the same time, God's love is demanding. "He that does not take up his cross and follow me is not worthy of me." On the one hand, God's love is first. On the other hand, God demands all from those to whom He has given all. His love is not that distortion of love, conditional love, which is not really love at all. Conditional love says, "I will love you if you meet this condition or that." This is a counterfeit love.

On the other hand, God's love is not indulgence either. Indulgence is also something other than love. When we are indulged, we do nothing but take, take, take. Indulgent "love" stymies growth as much as conditional "love." The two qualities that come through the relationship of unconditional love are security and the need to contribute of ourselves. And these are central qualities for growth for sanctification. It is in God's giving us His love to start with that we receive our security. Security is knowing that we are loved for ourselves. And it is this security that is the *basis* for growth. At the same time, we are called upon to contribute ourselves—to give of ourselves. Contributing is the *means* for growth.

II.

Sanctification has a direct relationship to family living.
Somebody has said when a person becomes a Christian, even his dog should be the better for it. Sometimes the dog is better off but nobody else in the family is. It is in the family setting where our Christian profession should be experienced. But it is very difficult to carry through here, as you well know. I am sure there have been times in your family which you would like to forget. Those clashes—those hot wars or cold wars that have been in your family. You would like to wipe them out of your memory, but you know very well that when you return home this summer, it could all happen again.

But you say, "It won't happen when I establish my own family!" Famous last words! It *can* happen because of our simulation of previous patterns in our family roles. You are very good now at picking out your parents' good points and bad points and you are determined never to duplicate what you consider their faults. But these are precisely what you will duplicate in your own parenthood role. In that split second moment when the conditions are reminiscent you will react—without even thinking, in the way your own parents would have reacted under the same circumstances. This is the pattern you have seen for twenty years. When you are in that role, you will follow through with this pattern of parental behavior unless there is some decided work done to prevent it.

The family is the place where we let down our hair. And this is not always a very nice thing to behold. When we let our hair down, we may let our worst out. In spite of this the goal in family relationships is the deepening of the tie of love between family members. And the goal in our sanctification is also a deepening of the tie of love between God our Heavenly Father and us. God's love has come to me in the sacrifice and suffering of His Son. This evokes a response of love from me. "We love because He first loved us." When the sinner beholds his God in the person of Jesus Christ suffering for his redemption, a response goes out from that sinner—a gratitude and a love to the God who has given Himself for him. But this love is indiscriminate. You can not love here and not love there. This would be an automatic contradiction of love. "He who loves God loves his brother also."

The church is the company of the redeemed that is called out by this love. So the church is the fellowship of believers who have received this love of God and have in turn been moved to respond to God and to their neighbor with this same love. So the church both gives this love of God and stimulates this love from others in its own fellowship and to all mankind. This is why we call the church the body of Christ. It is what the world sees of Christ because it is what the world experiences of Christ's love. The church is a family—the family of God. The ties between the members of the church are spiritual. In this family of God, there is the smaller unit, the biological family. But the biological family in the church is also tied with spiritual ties, as the love of Christ exists between the members of the family.

The implications for family living are spelled out for us in the Scriptures. This idea of love is a rather vague something or other. We do not know quite what we mean in the English language when we talk about love. But there is no doubt about what the Scriptural understanding of *Christian* love is. St. Paul spells it out in unmistakable terms in I. Cor. 13: "Love is patient and kind; love is not arrogant or rude; love is not irritable or resentful; love is not jealous or boastful; love does not insist on its own way; love bears all things, believes all things, hopes all things, endures all things."

III.

This unconditional love that we have been talking about is the basis for family security. As each person in the family is accepted by the other members of the family on the basis of his person rather than on the basis of his achievements, he is helped to grow—to feel that he really belongs to the family unit. It is on this same basis that we have our security with our heavenly Father. We are not loved by God because we are lovable, but we become lovable because we are loved. The same principle works in the family setting. Even as I understand the earthly pattern better by understanding the heavenly pattern of the family relationships, so the earthly pattern of our family relationships can color our understanding of the heavenly. People may be blocked in receiving this love from God by an earthly relationship which has gotten in the way. Our own parental relationships are to some extent imperfect since everybody is imperfect. We have a tendency to project onto God the mental picture we have developed from our human relationships, particularly our paternal relationships. Therefore, God must break through the picture we have of Him to reveal His real self. Our picture of Him is partially distorted by those human relationships that remind us of God, and which we cast onto God's image in our minds. As Fritz Kunkel has said:

> The child cannot yet distinguish between the parents and God. To him the parents are God. The love for man and the love for God are identical. Subjectively, the child does not realize that there is a choice. He accepts his parents as they are and applies what he learns from them to life and mankind and God. They are his encyclopaedic knowledge of religion. Here is the point where religious education begins. If we destroy the early group feeling of our children, we destroy the basis of their religious faith. If we are bad parents, the child learns that God is bad.

IV.

This is a responsibility upon parents that can lead the conscientious parent to despair. Parental guilt is most severe. I can assure you if you have ever felt guilty about some of your relationships with your parents, although your parents will never let you know, they have exceeded you in their experience of guilt over these same difficulties. This is particularly true in our age. No matter what magazine you pick up, from *Harpers* to the *Ladies Home Journal* you will find an article about how to be a better parent. Parents are reading these articles; they are discussing them with each other; they are discussing them in the PTA and in the church. The whole idea seems to be that if you do not watch out—if you do not do just the right thing—you will ruin your child. We want our children to grow up normal so we can feel better about having been good parents. We want to become more confident about the job we are doing. So it is for our sakes that our children must turn out well.

But this may seem too much for us. So we have today the age of the anxious parent—the parent with that heavy touch because there is too much at stake. By his anxiety the parent is showing the very unacceptance that he wishes to avoid. By his anxiety over the child he shows the child he does not really have confidence in him . . . therefore, he must manipulate the child so that the child will come out right. The child is viewed more as an "it"—a thing—than a person. He is something we are fashioning rather than a person in his own right from whom we also can learn. Pastoral Theologian Reuel Howe puts it this way: "All these books on parenthood tell me that all my child needs is my love. That is great! For just when my child needs my love, I find him most unlovable!"

For this cause the parent's growth is necessary for the children's growth. Elton Trueblood in his book, *The Recovery of Family Life*, which he wrote with his wife, says:

The parent makes the mistake, frequently, of concentrating on the child, when he would help the child more if he would concentrate on himself. The parent must guard, accordingly against the danger of too much self-sacrifice. If the sacrifice is obvious it defeats its purpose. Much as we help those whom we love by performing services for them, we help them more by being composed and happy persons. More good is done in personal relations by the habit of happiness than by obvious deeds of kindness.

The book of Proverbs would agree: "A cheerful heart is a good medicine." A cheerful heart is a good medicine in family relations. Horace Bushnell, the early American educator of our country expressed it this way:

If the child is handled fretfully, scolded or jerked or simply laid aside unaffectionately, in no warmth of motherly gentleness, it feels the sting of just that which is felt towards it; and so it is angered by anger, irritated by irritation, fretted by fretfulness; having thus impressed just that kind of impatience of ill-nature which is felt towards it, and growing faithfully into the bad mold offered as by a fixed law.

V.

In the frustration over their own growth, parents may demand too much of their children. Those of you whose parenthood is still in the future could well ponder this as a reality in life. In the frustration over our own growth we try to transfer this growth to our children. We begin what the Phillips's paraphrase of Ephesians calls "overcorrecting." The more dissatisfied with ourselves we are, the more we try to correct our mistakes in our children. This hypercritical attitude either creates the broken spirit conformist who rebels (if he can rebel at all) in a hidden way because he has too much at stake to rebel outwardly, or it creates the angry rebel who cannot conform at all because if he does, he is giving up the fight for his own personality.

We have a way of demanding from our children what we cannot do ourselves. It is rather easy to see this when you stand outside of your own family circle. It is much more difficult to see it in your own circle. Watch on occasion when the children begin to fight. The parents quickly put a stop to it: "Cut it out! What's the matter with you kids!" But how the kids have to watch Mother and Dad go at it with no holds barred—at least verbally. Also, when the kids begin complaining about the things in the home—about the way Mother and Dad operate, they are told: "Stop that! No more complaining! What's the matter with you?" But how the children have to listen to Mother and Dad complain about the grandparents, or about other in-laws, or about the neighbors, or about the church, or about the pastor. I find myself most critical and rejecting towards my children when they seem to show what I know are my own weaknesses. One of our directors of a Lutheran children's home in Iowa was asked during a conference by a parent, "How long will it take me to teach my children to turn the other cheek?" He replied, "Madam, how long has it taken you?" We want our children to be perfect in proportion to our inability to accept our own imperfection.

VI.

But there are those moments when it all seems to fall apart —when frustration comes, and despair, and defeat, and even bitterness in defeat. We become discouraged with our family, discouraged with our marriage, discouraged with our children—and the children become discouraged with their parents, discouraged over their home, ashamed of their home. Yet here, too, our family relationships relate to our sanctification. According to the Scriptures, we are sanctified by being crucified with Christ and being resurrected to the new man. In this way, as Luther pointed out, we relive our baptism. Each day we die to the old Adam and are resurrected to the new man. Dying is painful, and if it is not painful, it is not dying. So the way of growth is not a smooth upward way.

It is a way of dips and rises, and every rise is followed by a dip. The dip brings on the struggles with realities that otherwise we might ignore. Out of this struggle comes the rise to a higher level than before.

Family living is very good at supplying these dips! You know that! You know how terrible you can feel in some of the dips in your own family relations; how terrible you feel about your own behavior in some of these family conflicts. But this is a responsibility from which we do not withdraw as an impediment to our spiritual life because it is demanding and is defeating. Because the pattern for our growth is by way of crucifixions and resurrections, we can see why family living can lead to even higher sanctification than withdrawing from it. It supplies the dips the Holy Spirit uses to crucify our old Adam so that we are conformed to the image of Christ by the purging of our pride. Failure and defeat are painful, but they are the way to the resurrection—to victory and growth. If anything keeps one humble, it is his behavior pattern in his own family circle. And humility is one of the essence of sanctification. If anything should convince one that he is justified by grace alone, it is his record in his own family relationships.

The Church's ministry of reconciliation has its direct influence in family living. Here is where relationships are estranged. Reconciliation in the smaller unit, the family, is similar to reconciliation in the larger unit, the congregation. Instead of being in remorse and despair over our family failures—or even defensively trying to justify ourselves in our family role—we are given hope to repent. For repentance is sorrow with hope, and repentance leads to reunion. If I would define a Christian home, it would not be a home where everyone is perpetually nice to every one else. I would not know where such a home exists. Rather, I would define a Christian home as a home where the spirit of forgiveness reigns between husband and wife and between parents and children, between children and parents and between children and children. For we all need it.

This viewpoint ties in all of life with our sanctification. It also creates hope where otherwise we might despair. It offers the resurrection of hope through trust in God—that He is greater than our blunders, even greater than our sins. This helps us as parents to leave room for the Heavenly Parent in our relationships with our children, where otherwise we might get in His way. He may succeed with our children even when we fail. Trust in God helps us to develop the lighter touch with our children. The saints of God are known for not taking themselves too seriously. Child psychology is a great help. It prepares us for the stages in a child's development that otherwise might catch us off guard. But by itself, child psychology puts all the burden on our shoulders. And this is too much!

Faith in God helps us to see beyond our present family crises—our involvement in family-centered guilt, anger, anxiety, and discouragement—the one thing needful. It helps us to regain our balance so that we might better fulfill our role. With our mate, our children, and our parents—as with God, "we walk not by sight, but by faith."

DR. HAROLD B. KILDAHL, JR.
Pastor, First Lutheran Church, Minot, North Dakota

DR. KILDAHL gave this address at the Commencement Exercises for the Class of 1961 on May 28, 1961.

Assignment Tomorrow

PRESIDENT EASTVOLD, members of the Board of Regents, honored guests, members of the faculty, graduating Seniors, parents, students, friends.—To remark that my presence here today is an honor I prize highly, is to observe what must be obvious. To join you on the occasion of your first commencement exercise following the achievement of University status and to share for the moment in the affairs of this institution which represents an educational adventure of daring and enterprise—physically, scholastically and spiritually—is both thrilling and exhilarating for me. To be privileged by bestowed honor to join the Alumni of Pacific Lutheran University is one of my life's most rewarding moments. I have the desire, but not the intention, to recount the recent history of this University, and as a member of the responsible Board of College Education of The American Lutheran Church, I join with thousands of others who have prayed and supported this cause, in expressing amazement and astonishment at what has taken place on this campus in the passage of a few years. Dr. Eastvold—you, your faculty, and administrative personnel have the enthusiastic admiration and gratitude of us all. Your leadership at Pacific Lutheran University has had dramatic results. We are most thankful for this adventure in sound Christian education. But, no evidence of what has taken place here can equal the evidence presented physically before this platform today as the 1961 graduating class prepares to move into a new and demanding phase of life. Call it "Assignment Tomorrow"—to roll back the edges of life.

The edges of life that you, graduating Seniors, have encountered in a theoretical way, and which you will shortly meet in a vital way are somewhat jagged and torn. There is little about this present world and life in it that is either smooth or static. Time, and certainly not the least, time in this present moment, is always charged with dynamics, movement that challenges the imagination, knowledge and efforts of men. In the present, when we are required to shift our whole frame of reference and our attention away from "products to processes, from properties to characteristics, from causality to purpose," and we realize that the human family is doubling its storehouse of knowledge every ten years—so fast, in fact, that some areas of knowledge are practically unteachable—you, the prepared youth of the nation and your young colleagues the world around, are faced with the demand for heroic adventure as you roll back the edges of life—the jagged edges—to discover, what will most certainly be discovered, a new format and basis of life in which and by which men of earth can and will live at peace with one another, a new concept of society in which law and world government will govern the ways of men.

But there are those who say to you that you are entering a world in which the visible and subtle signs of decay and crumbling foundations combine to discourage and dismay the adventurous spirit. Prophets of woe are contending with their voices raised in stern warning to announce what they believe must surely be the final curtain drawn across the stage of time. "Look!" they shout. "The world of men is a rebellious world, with whole continents in revolt—the conclusion will be nuclear warfare on a universal scale. The end is in sight." "Look," they shout; "what promised to be a forum for the nations of the earth at the United Nations is failing; gladiatorial thrusts are made at the tower of the U.N. and it appears that the world will once again be turned into a giddy whirl, with chaos the predictable result." "Look," they shout, "the threat of Communism and its spread of foul and dastardly ideological half-truths and untruths has broken through the protective walls of the Monroe Doctrine and has invaded the West, threatening the very life of the United States and the Latin-American nations. There is no avoiding it, America will shortly be reduced to a second rate status." "Look," they shout, "the shadow of a governmental hand is fallen on education, medical and hospital care, and the sensitive areas of business, industry, labor —the tax structure is killing—we shall surely be a welfare state—and soon."

With the prophets of woe the critics of culture are joined, and they too warn the adventurous to be aware of the breakdown in the moral, ethical and spiritual fabric that once was America. "Only tatters," they say, "remain of what was once a beautiful fabric." "Observe," they say, "the inflationary spiral in which we are caught, which will destroy the wealth of the nation and isolate this economy from the rest of the world." "Observe," they say, "the contemporary literary scene, the motion picture industry, the plight of television, the pressures for legalized gambling, the exorbitant national liquor bill, the instability of the family, the 'crack in the picture window' of suburbia, the decline of social institutions and respect for law—all of this clearly indicates that we are at the end of a moral, ethical, spiritual rope, exhausting our strength trying to hang on, and only a suicidal fall awaits us." "Observe," they say—"the

Christian church is drifting away from its traditional and confessional moorings and is flirting with soft psychological devices and means for lulling people to sleep in the happy contentment of possessing a 'chummy God.' " "Conclude with us," they say, "that the only real concern of the American people is a materialistic one—more things, gadgets, comforts, ease, entertainment—with a declining interest in participating in anything that requires effort, energy or expenditure. The major concern of the American people is simply—'after two cars—what?' " The prophets of woe and the critics of culture would have you believe that the world into which you go is one in which the best you can do is to seek the serenity of solitude and time to lick your wounds before the end will come. "Take your choice—be beat or angry—there is nothing more." And, having thus declared themselves, they look longingly at yesterday, and the glory of the "good old days" become an impregnable fortress from which flies the banner of a lost cause.

But, I refuse to join them—I refuse to be identified with the siren's song that sings of despair. I want to live with my head erect, with my heart beating high, with a quickened footstep, with the edges of tomorrow the bold adventure to which I take my confident stride. I would not escape from reality, but with courage I would encounter and grapple with it. I invite you to grapple with the edges of life, and win through. Such is the assignment of tomorrow—your assignment.

North—far North—on the shores of Great Slave Lake, in the Arctic region, a new village has recently been planted. It bears the colorful name of YELLOW KNIFE. It is a little place that serves adventurous men as a base of operations as they methodically explore the remaining one million square miles of trackless tundra in search of gold. Gold was discovered at Yellow Knife and people have moved in, houses have been built, mines have been opened, and gold is sluiced from the earth. The edges of civilization are being rolled back as men pit their intelligence, their skill and daring against the caprice of nature. It is not men who will emerge the fallen; it is the environment that will fall captive to the skills of men. Nature itself will return captive as life invades and holds that forbidding land.

Yellow Knife is but a symbol of the realms of life that are now hidden by the jagged, torn edges which will be rolled back by the youth of this day.

Let no man deceive you with empty words. There are problems—great and sundry problems—in science and discovery, in international relations and human affairs, in moral and social life, in the mastery of man himself, and his motivations—these, and countless related problems await your skills and patience. There are no longer any easy problems, nor any easy solutions. The international atmosphere is charged with volatile components, and lethargy often appears to grip the minds and imaginations of men. Yet, the time is at hand, I earnestly believe, when a major breakthrough in human relations must occur, when the cultural barriers separating peoples must be broken. And, its quest and goal must certainly be the conquest of peace—ultimately to discover the pattern and the form, as well as the rule of peace. We need to ask ourselves—How long can we permit the refugees of the world to constitute a threat to the peace of the world—to be the pawns on the International chessboard? How long can we enjoy the comforts that are ours, and be half-heartedly concerned with the rooftop dwellers of Hong Kong, with whom I visited just a week ago—men and women who have lost everything but a flickering hope—the displaced peoples of Jordan, who, after twelve years of armistice still present a desperate cause for concern; the uprooted families of India and Western Europe, the Congolese miner who is earning a paltry thirty dollars a year? How long can we ignore the existence of Red China with its 700,000,000 people, when we realize that in a decade that figure will rise to one billion, and by the year 2050, sixty per cent of the people of the world will be Chinese? There, in the isolated nation of Chinese, where only ten years ago one million youth were in high school, today more than fifteen million are enrolled. There,

100,000,000 children are attending elementary schools. There, the invasion of universities has been revolutionary. How long can we regard the United Nations as a theory and not a fact? How long can national autonomy prevail as men ignore the actual existence of universal moral law? How long can we tolerate a gigantic conspiracy against freedom and the encirclement of free men by the Red pincer movement? The daring and prepared youth of today have rich veins in which to mine the real gold of the world—the gold of human relations, which will most assuredly be the wealth of the nations. We dare not dream of universal law and the brotherhood of nations if we refuse to pit our intelligence and skill in effecting the dream. We dare not avoid the responsibilities of privilege. The exciting call to youth in The Peace Corps, now in infancy, is an encouraging development which will send trained and screened men and women to foreign countries to share with them knowledge, skill and methods. In Latin America the median age is just 21.5 years, and any 4-H member could teach a South American farmer how to raise improved crops. The Strategic Services Corps—just now advanced by William Lederer, in his book, *A Nation of Sheep,* published two weeks ago—is another daring suggestion for individual participation in the quest for peace. These are only two of the current suggestions reaching for fulfillment, which give a thrill to being young today—to be a member of the generation that enters this golden age of opportunity. Upon the youth of the world—here and abroad—hangs the responsibility and opportunity of a new world discovery. It is this very idea of personal commitment that gave birth to the exciting World Brotherhood Exchange program now in infancy.

In this golden age of opportunity I see the blue skies receding into purple, and then to black, as the farther reaches of space are probed. The light of the sun reaches the earth in just eight minutes, but the light of the nearest star requires four years to reach the earth. Space—now punctuated by the eery "beeb-beeb-beeb" of the satellites drifting in orbit, by the noise of machines carrying men through space at the rate of forty miles a minute, by the sounds of electronically controlled capsules hurtling toward Venus and to orbit around the sun, by the exploits of a Russian Gargarin, and an American Alan Shephard, staggers the imagination of men. It is no longer nonsense to ask, "Who owns the moon?" The future is enormous—with space secrets finally known, with that edge of life rolled back in a splendid effort to bring peace finally to the world of men—for surely none can escape the fact that the consciousness of the realms of space must most assuredly produce the consciousness of our need for each other. It is a strange fact that a patient flying over Honolulu with transducers attached to his body can be accurately diagnosed by a group of physicians in Montgomery, Alabama, watching a television receiver. The space age presents a rich vein in which to mine the gold that is truly the wealth of nations—the gold of universality and the brotherhood of man. Peace—this is the goal men have always sought, and today—around the world—men are demanding more and more protection from the diabolical destructive powers of the war potentials, that an era of peace may finally dawn upon the earth.

In the world of tomorrow men will live to be a hundred and twenty years or more. A medical break-through will shortly occur. Cancer will be defeated—the mystery of the heart will be understood—the chemistry of the blood will no longer be a riddle—dietary needs of men will be a basic science—paper and plastics will take the place of many fabrics and materials—adhesives will replace nails and screws and ordinary building materials—we will fly at the rate of 1,200 miles an hour, and buy our pre-packaged foods with heating units built in; teaching machines will be in common use; giant computers will be used by experts to accurately predict events to come. The new Golden Age will dawn, and you will be a part of it, and all of the discoveries and changes that occur will bring men a little closer to each other in understanding and sympathy and love for one another. What a thrill it is to enter the world where opportunity awaits every man to roll back the jagged edges of life in search for the pure gold—the age of peace.

In this Golden Age man himself will need to be explored and understood. His emotions and deep spiritual recesses, his mind and extra-sensory perceptions, creativity, and his soul—all will be better understood. And this is the great need of tomorrow. Men need to know that when they look at a man they must see more than his eyes and ears, or the twinkle in his eye, or the frown that he wears; they must learn to see him for what he is—a brother; a creation of God, endowed with the Divine image, for whom a cross was once carried to a hill.

The hope of such discovery lies in youth—youth, who, like you, have been exposed to the mysteries of science, and the magic of nature's wonders, to the unraveled story of yesterday, to the exciting gymnastics of the philosopher's mind, to the unlocked strongbox of other tongues, but who have also been exposed to the highest wisdom man is commissioned to communicate, which is the fear of the Lord.

You, the students exiting from this place, must carry with you the assurance that God lives—that life is His special province; that Christ redeems all men and the world itself; that the worth of a man is not to be computed in terms of what he is or what he has, but in terms of what, by God's grace, he can be—more than a physical giant who scales the peak of Everest, more than an intellectual giant who leaves the world the legacy of *The Republic,* more than a scientific giant who devises intricate machines for the invasion of the moon, more than a creative giant, who, with pen in hand, writes and composes Beethoven's "Seventh," more than a towering genius or a dedicated mad-man who searches for a conscious machine; but that man can be a child of God—his heart beating high with love for God, his eyes filled with the glory of the coming of the Lord, the redeemed potential of heaven. THIS is the mission of high hope—the great adventure, the edge of tomorrow that needs desperately to be rolled back in the search for gold—the gold of the Spirit of God at work in the hearts of men. This is "Assignment: Tomorrow."

You stand at the edges of tomorrow—some offer you condolences as you cross the edges fraught with danger; but I offer you cheers, for you bring with you hope for a better day.

Today is the birthday anniversary of a great man of long ago—Anselm, by name—born in 1033. He played a large role in dispelling the fears and superstitions of men. In his book, *Concerning Truth,* he wrote: "Flee now for a little while your accustomed occupations; hide yourselves for a brief moment from your tumultuous thoughts; cast aside your cares, postpone your toilsome engagements; devote yourselves a while to God; repose in Him, and enter the sanctuary of your soul. Then, within the closed doors of your retirement, inquire after your God." I commend this act to you and your concern, that you may be well prepared for the adventure of another day.

At Yellow Knife the daring of men has opened a new frontier, and the edges of life have been rolled back. I greet you at the edges of your life waiting to be rolled back. Be not discouraged, frustrated, defeated by the ragged edges that meet your eye, but, by the help of God, young men and women, roll them back and discover the new and glorious day that awaits discovery tomorrow. This is the assignment—tomorrow awaits you, and your daring thrust in the quest for peace.

To you, Dr. Eastvold, my thanks on behalf of many, for the fruitful years you have given to Christian Education, to your Church, to Pacific Lutheran University. To you, men and women of the faculty, my admiration, on behalf of many, for your consecrated service to God and man. To you, graduates, my congratulations and cheers. On you, and millions like you, Assignment Tomorrow depends for its fulfillment. Godspeed—and His blessing be upon you.

DR. S. C. EASTVOLD
President, Pacific Lutheran University

DR. EASTVOLD gave this address at Baccalaureate
Services for the Class of 1961 on May 28, 1961.

"And He Shall Be Like a Tree Planted"

—Psalm 1:3

DEARLY BELOVED, Graduating Class of our University Year
and assembled friends—Grace and Peace!

Our text comes from the Psalm which has been placed
first in the collection because, from its general character
and subject, it forms a suitable introduction to the entire
Book of Psalms. It treats of the blessedness of the righteous
and the misery of the wicked—topics which constantly recur
in the Psalms—but it treats of them as if all experiences
point in one direction. The moral problem, which, in other
Psalms, troubles the ancient poets of Israel when they see
evil prospering and the good depressed, has no place here.
The poet rests calmly in the truth that it is well with the

righteous. He is not vexed with those passionate questions of heart which meet us in such Psalms as the 37th and 73rd. Hence, we may probably conclude that his lot was cast in happier and more peaceful times.

We are at the close of spring time. It has been tree planting time. Arbor Day has been observed across the nation. We have enjoyed the wonder, the miracle, the ever-new delight of a wonderful season.

Nature has opened her outdoor pleasure garden and the birds and the bees and flowers are with us. Weeks ago there were tokens and forerunners. Who can tell the first signs of spring? The swollen buds of the pussy willows, the bee crawling slowly up and down the great trunk of the sugar maple—all these are certain hints. As soon as Dame Nature throws off her shy, cold airs and coyly unveils her woodland beauty, we hear the cry that goes up from every living thing—from growing plant, weed and flower, from bug and butterfly, from bee and bird. It is the cry of invitation, "Come out into the world of fresh air and sunshine! Come out and join us in the song of the open road."

Does not all of this seem like a parable for this graduating class as you hear the call of service in the spring time of your lives?

In all of nature, there is scarcely a living thing that has so many lessons for us as "TREES."

THE CHRISTIAN MAN IS LIKE A TREE—PLANTED!

HE IS LIKE A TREE

Every airplane that crosses California's mighty mountain system, the Sierra-Nevada, may soar above the giant Sequoias or Bigtrees. This tree is not just *a* big tree—it is *the* big tree of all the world. Donald Culross Peattie, writing in the *"Mainliner"* (May, 1961), a magazine published for the United Air Lines guests, writes eloquently about these Bigtrees (used by permission). He says they are the oldest and most ponderous of all living things. There are taller trees on earth, but all other trees cannot rival the girth, or the diameter, or age of the Bigtrees of California. Their home is at an altitude of between 4,000 and 8,000 feet above sea level, on the western slopes of the Sierra. Today their numbers are reduced to some 26 isolated groves. Some, accessible by road, are visited by millions annually; others not easily reached, small and remote, are never seen except by some forest ranger making his rounds. Never do these trees grow isolated, rather always in a rejoicing company of their own kind.

And what a company! Among the spectacular aged giants, you see the groves of tiny seedlings shining as young trees, as promising as fair children. The growth is swift for the first few centuries, but they slow down as the girth becomes greater. The life of these giant trees stretch back for thirty centuries of upright, lofty, green growing impressiveness. The pure snows drift against them, but the deepest drifts merely wrap the ankles of the giants' 271, even 281, feet in height. The sunlight flashes from the tiny scale-like leaves; the pileated woodpeckers knock on the boles with a lordly racket in the forest silence; and Douglas squirrels skip impudently out on the farthest, most perilous branches to nip off the cones. There is no gloom in the presence of the Bigtrees. They stand side by side as the trunks of the oldsters let the sunshine in.

Almost laughably small are the cones of these giants of the earth, and so tiny are the flaky seeds that, to make up one ounce of them, it takes 3,000, and the kernel of each seed is only one-quarter of an inch long. Yet inside this is embodied the embryo of the future titan.

The mind of man, reflecting the intelligence of God, is likened to a tree. Here in the seed of the Bigtree of California is the power of growth, that awes the visitor—it is a peaceful power, a promising power.

Like the tiny seed which produces the titanic monarch of the forest, so the regenerated man bespeaks an eternal endurance, too, for he bespeaks the endless seasons which weather the winds and storms. If these Bigtrees, in their babyhood, escape the armies of cutworms and black ants that then attack them, as well as the browsing of black-tailed deer, they are good for a lifetime of centuries. Very low in resin content, so thickly clad in a rugged bark, hardly less resistant to flames than asbestos, they usually come through a raging forest fire, not without scars, but living vigorously still.

And, like the Christian man, the Bigtree is almost without commercial use, unlike its sister on the coast. Early lumbermen did not know this, and they made a great attack upon what may have been the finest stand of the Bigtree, at Converse Basin. But the giants, when felled, hit the earth with such a blow of hundreds of tons, that the brittle wood shattered and, worse, it broke against the grain.

So it was when Adam and Eve fell in the garden of Eden. God in His mercy came in to rescue a great forest of Bigtrees, and they now stand under the protection of His Grace. God came to man's rescue by setting up the Cross, a great wooden tree, and there He produced a redemptive power, thus setting man aside from complete exploitation. Since that power has come to the world, the Christian man, like a Bigtree in God's forest, is all but immune from attack from insect, animal or satanic buzz saw. As he grows to maturity, he never dies from spiritual disease or decay. The only thing that can destroy this tree, or shake him from his earthly rooting, is the divine bolt of lightning which cleaves him from the earth—in this sense he prefers to perish from the earth by an Act of God, and be transplanted into his Heavenly Home.

The man-tree looks upward. He is an optimist who seeks all the light he can get, always seeking to live where the air is clearest and the conditions are best.

Like the apple tree, the biggest ones grow in the top branches. So the Christian man lives the richest life by reaching up into the light where he can look into God's face,

There are trees that plant themselves. The mangrove tree is possibly the only tree in the world that has the sense and the power to plant itself. The fruit of this strange member of treedom is about the size of an ordinary pear, and, tucked away inside of it, is one small seed. In that one seed there is imprisoned an important and impatient treelet, that cannot wait to be planted in the ordinary way, but begins to grow while it is still inside the fruit. The first real hot spell of weather brings out slender roots from every pear hanging on the mangrove tree, and these tiny white strings begin to grow so fast that, in an amazingly short time, they are several feet long. But a slight wind knocks the fruit off, and, as they strike the ground, the big ripe pears open, freeing the little sprouted seeds, which at once begin to burrow down into the earth with the ends of their long roots, so that before long, all about the parent tree will be seen a thriving forest. In this sense, we should grow thoughts and habits that will plant themselves and grow.

But we are concerned with the tree that God plants. The mightiest trees are of His planting. Culture and training of our powers are to be valued and sought, but the noblest traits of character must be gained by direct communion with God. Every breath of air may stir the leaves, but a tree itself that is firmly rooted is unmoved by the fiercest storms. The only life that can hold up steadfastly against all trials and temptations is one whose roots take hold of eternal truths that cannot be shaken.

In the province of God, some trees are cut from the spiritual forest as they mature, leaving the small trees to grow up. Without the care of God, all the trees in this spiritual forest would be destroyed. Thus there is a powerful agent in this spiritual conservation. God holds a constant watch against the enormous evils that seek to waste His plantings.

In spite of increasing costs in the Christian homes, the Christian schools, colleges and seminaries, this spiritual forest has been preserved. As time has passed, this forest has become ever more valuable and productive, instead of disappearing altogether.

God has called us to be partners in spiritual tree planting. He who plants a tree for shade or to beautify his property, provides not only for his own comfort, but for the comfort and welfare of posterity. He plants for the future, as for the present; for others, as for himself.

WHERE DOES THIS TREE GROW?

This man is like a tree planted by brooks of water. The usual name in Hebrew for streams is "brooks," as in Arabic and Ethiopic, because brooks and streams cleave and divide the surface of the earth. The double plural refers partly to the abundance of water, which is very important in the Orient; partly to the rich distribution of brooks for the fructification of every tree of that kind. The Psalmist alludes to those brooks which, having their source in some perennial fountain, flow through the wadies and valleys, fertilizing the land wherever these brooks are found; their banks are crowded with a rich luxuriance of plants and trees.

These brooks were diverted into many channels in order that their blessings might be more widely diffused. Its waters are divided into a hundred water courses, using every drop of water to fertilize a hundred villages.

This is symbolic of the perennial fountain of life—an allusion to the garden of Eden and the Tree of Life in it. The water of life of the Divine Word produces the sap and strength which gradually ripens and spreads the blessings of God in the world.

THE FRUIT EXPECTED FROM THIS TREE

Every tree has its own type of manifestation.

The oak roars, the beech shrieks, the elm has a deep groan, the ash moans, the pine whistles, the birch sighs, the mulberry sings, and the willow whispers. These strains combine to make the great choir of mankind.

Some men are like the oak in strength and steadfastness, others like the elm, for shade and shelter. Some are like the hickory, for unyieldingness; others are like the grand sequoias for majesty, grandeur and genius; some are like the willow in sorrow and suffering, while others are like the myrtle trees that clap their hands for joy. Some are fruitful in deeds of benevolence and kindness, others are barren as the boughs of winter. Some are changeable as the seasons; others are as perennial as the evergreen.

Like the trees, so the Christian man gives his fruit in his season. In such a case, expectation is never disappointed. *The fruit comes when it should come!*

A godly education, under the influence of the Holy Spirit, is sure to produce the fruits of righteousness. He who reads, prays and meditates will *see* the work which God has given him to do; he will experience the *power* by which to perform it; and he will *see* the *places* and *opportunities* for doing God's will. Such a man must join the impatient person at the pool of Bethesda and step in when the angel stirs the water. When this man is under temptations, he will lean on the Lord; when he is given dignity and power, he will consider what God requires at such a time. A wise husbandman of God hath his distinct employments, bringing forth his fruit in every season.

This blessed man, being free at all times, in all places, for every work, will serve whenever an opportunity is afforded him. He is neither a Jew, nor a Gentile, nor a Greek, nor a Barbarian. Martin Luther said of this man, "He gives his fruits in his season. Therefore his fruits have no name, and his times have no name."

"His leaf also shall not wither." He describes the fruit before he does the leaf. The kingdom of God does not stand in word, but in power. About Jesus it was said, "Which was a prophet mighty in deed and word" (Luke 24:10). And thus, let him who professes the word of doctrine, first put forth the fruits of life, if he would not have his fruit to

134

wither, for Christ cursed the fig tree which bore no fruit.

The Lord's trees are all evergreens. No winter's cold can destroy their virtue; and yet, unlike the evergreens in our country, they are all fruit bearers while living.

Thousands of trees that are most carefully tended would hardly receive a moment's thought were it not for their fruit. It is the fruit that decides whether the tree is good or bad, worth keeping, or fit only for firewood. It is for their fruit that life is given to them; it is by their fruit that they are judged.

The godly man is known by the beneficence of his life. If we delight in God's law, He will fit us for the sphere and season in which we live, and make us a blessing to our generations.

The godly man is known by his character. As the foliage of the tree is its beauty and glory, so shall delight in the law of God give grace and majesty to the character. In inner rectitude is the secret of all true and visible excellence; out of a heart right with God springs all the poetry and utilities of life.

Since this man is a *transplanted* tree, he is not left to the efforts of nature, but is taken beneath the gardener's care and placed in a very favorable soil. He is not righteous by nature, or through his own power, skill, or activity, but by the Divine Agency through the *means of grace*. May God take us from the wilds of nature, graft us into Christ, nourish us by the influence of the Holy Spirit, and thus shall we bear our fruit unto holiness, and in the end, everlasting life.

LESSONS TAUGHT US BY THE TREES

Nature affords many lessons for the spiritual life. When the Master walked on earth, a *Man* among men, He gathered His illustrations from the objects around Him—the sky, the trees, the birds, the flowers, from all of which He drew words of comfort or reproof. From the lilies about His feet, the Master drew His most beautiful illustration and taught lessons of faith and love that have comforted many a tired soul. As the pure white lily grows out of the black soil, so man can rise above his environment and be pure in an impure world. From a pure life comes a sweet fragrance and an atmosphere that is inspiring.

None of the really good trees aspire to have a distinction above the others. They are content to remain in the place where their Creator has put them. The lofty Bigtree does not boast itself above those that are small and tender, but rather flings its arms around them to shelter them. This is true *humility*.

Each tree feels it has an office to fulfill, which is specially given to it to do, and which it must not leave undone. This is a true sense of *responsibility*.

Trees teach us a lesson of *hospitality*. They live with doors open to birds, to insects, to squirrels and to human beings. A naturalist estimated that one great tree entertained more guests of various kinds than the Waldorf-Astoria, and without money and without price.

There is no rebellion among the trees against the authority of Him Who appointed them their places, and assigned them their duties. That which is scantily laden, or bears a more common sort of fruit, does not murmur because it is not covered with rich clusters; but each seems content to bear that which is expected of it. It is obedient and submissive.

No tree wishes to despoil another tree of its glory. There is no joining together of those that are less favorite against those that are renowned for fertility and beauty. There is neither a strife for precedence, nor do the others show jealousy, if anyone is likely to have the precedence. So ought it to be among men of all classes, but especially among those who form a Christian University or the Church of God. All should feel that they have the same nature, are trees planted by the same hand, watered by the same clouds, and warmed by the same sun; and so, being united by many ties in common, should grow peaceably together as one vineyard of the Lord of hosts.

It is in but a secondary manner that any one tree derives benefits from another. One may to some extent protect another from the fury of the blasts, or contribute to it some of its heat, but all the primary conditions of health and strength of any tree belong to the soil in which it is placed, to the air around it, to the sun that shines upon it, and to the rain or dew that falls upon it. Its root must be fastened to the soil and on that everything depends in the first instance. The soil must be sufficient and rich in order to provide a luxuriant growth. The rain and dew must fall copiously and the sun must send forth heat.

In the spiritual vineyard, these conditions are essentially required. Fellow Christians may, in many ways, be helpful to each other, but each one is dependent for all that is primary on God alone. Each one is rooted by God's own hand in Christ, and built up in Him; and it is from Him that the rain and the dew of spiritual influences come down; it is He Who causes the Son of righteousness to rise with warmth and healing in His beams. The great practical lesson taught us by trees, therefore, is that the Christian's primary duty is to look after his relations to his God, and see that these are all right, for it is upon *that* that all which is essential to his growth depends.

To be useful is better than to reign. The fulfillment of one's vocation is far more important than to reign over others. To merely reign is to live for the glorification of oneself; to be useful is to be a fountainhead from which blessings might flow out to others. All the objects of Nature seem to say, "We exist *not* for ourselves, but for the benefit of others around us." The sun shines not for itself, but to enlighten and warm the planets that revolve around it. The clouds float in the firmament, not on their own account, but to distill their watery treasures on the thirsty ground. The birds sing among the branches and fill the grove with melody to give delight to the listening ears. The flowers put forth their blossoms, and convey a pleasing sense of view to the eye; the trees and shrubs grow and wave their branches in the breeze to glorify their Creator with the richness of their hues, the sweetness emitted by their fragrance, and by the excellence of the fruit they bear.

And what do trees teach materialistic America? "And whatsoever he doeth *shall prosper.*"

Let us take heed that we do not understand this to mean a *carnal* prosperity. This prosperity is a hidden prosperity, and lies entirely secret in spirit; and therefore if we do not have the prosperity which is by faith, we should rather judge any prosperity to be the greatest adversity. For as the devil bitterly hates this *"leaf"* and the Word of God, so he does also those who teach and hear it, and he persecutes such, aided by all the powers of the world. As Luther once said, "Therefore thou hearest of a miracle that is the greatest of all miracles, when thou hearest that all things prosper which a blessed man doeth." Here is the great blessing of an unwithered profession. Here are virtues exhibited at certain seasons—patience in affliction; gratitude in prosperity; and zeal in opportunity. Whatsoever he produceth shall come to maturity. Outward prosperity is sweet when it follows a close walking with God—as the cipher, when it follows a figure, adds to the number, though it be nothing in itself. This makes the wide difference between the righteous and the wicked. Man is either blessed or lost—so God's Word declares, so God's judgment warns. The pious and the wicked are together in this world; but their ways are entirely different from *beginning to end.* Man's lot is not determined by chance, but by righteous and infallible judgment. It is not enough to avoid this or that single sin, for we must walk in the *Way of Life.* He who would remain in the congregation of the righteous must *avoid* the society of the wicked, while he *must use diligently the means of grace* entrusted to the church of God. All things finally redound to the *salvation* of the righteous and the *destruction* of the wicked. The lot of the pious is as *delightful* as that of the wicked is *terrible.* Tell me the way in which you walk, and the company you keep, and I will declare to you the *end* which you will attain. The things in which you delight will either make you blessed or destroy you. Divine judgment comes *certainly,* strikes *surely,* judges *righteously,* and decides our *everlasting* weal or woe.

How shall we distinguish between the righteous and the wicked? The one *keeps* God's law with *delight,* the other *transgresses* it with *contempt;* the one associates with *scorners,* the other remains in the *congregation;* the one *prospers* with God's *assistance,* the other *perishes* by God's *judgment.*

To err and fail is human. But to continue in error and sin is the work of the devil. But there is a blessed way out of this dilemma: it is to hear and learn the Word of God and to freely and openly confess sin and receive Divine grace and pardon.

Today we all stand between two ways which lead to everlasting weal or woe. Let us open our eyes and choose the best. He who has nothing sure in heaven, can have nothing firm on earth. Permanent prosperity and happiness are to be found only in the ways of virtue and godliness. There is a curse wrapped up in the wicked man's prosperity, while there is a blessing concealed in the righteous man's crosses, losses and sorrows. The righteous man plows the furrows of earth and sows a harvest there which shall never be fully reaped until he enters the enjoyment of eternity; but for the wicked, he plows the sea, and though there may seem to be a shining trail behind his keel, yet the waves pass over it and the place that knew him shall know him no more forever. The very *"way"* of the ungodly shall perish.

Finally, it takes not only a fruit tree, but a tree with an unfading leaf, to picture a Christian. He is always flourishing: sorrows and afflictions, which are commonly thought to be misfortunes, may befall him often, but he has success so genuine that it cannot be marred by any or all of these. Dost thou not know, my friends, that a tree which grows to itself is more exposed to winds and storm than another that stands surrounded by other trees in the woods?

Nearly all trees shed their leaves each year. Even the evergreens shed their leaves. As the fresh leaves of the ever-

green are fully grown before the old leaves change, the fall
of the old ones is not noticed—the tree is always green; but
if you will look under the pine tree (which is an evergreen),
you will find the ground covered with long brown needles
which were once green leaves. Each tree, when it casts its
leaves, is left with buds which will swell and burst and
throw out new leaves.

The evergreen has its message—keep always fresh and
young. Don't get rusty. Don't lose your sympathy with youth
and the world. Keep young. *Be an evergreen Christian!*

LET US PRAY

Oh, Lord, we thank Thee for a day so sweet and fair as
this *University Year* Commencement day. Like the trees,
we lift up our hands in a psalm of gratitude to Thee. May
every little budding flower of faith be opened into a psalm
of gratitude of praise to Thee. We thank Thee for all Thine
handwritings of revelation on the walls of the world, on the
heavens above us in this marvelous space age, and on the
earth beneath, and for all the testimonials which record
Thy presence, Thy power, Thy justice, and Thy love. And
most of all, we thank Thee for the revelation of Thyself in
Thy precious Word, the Bible. May this University graduating class go out from among these ivy halls into the University of Hard Knocks, prepared to take their places beside
the sturdy trees that have gone before them. May they never
live unto themselves, but may they follow the rule that "it
is more blessed to give than to receive." In all of this, may
they have the abiding consciousness that they do not live
in vain, that they are not useless ciphers. Amen.

DATE DUE

DEC 5 '63			
FEB 2 1 '64			
DEC 1 3			
JUN 29 '67			
JUN 2 9 '67			
GAYLORD			PRINTED IN U.S.A.